Customer-Centric Business

How to Build a Business That Delights Customers and Drives Profits

DARREN HANSON

informational purposes solely, and is universal as so. The presentation of the information is without contract or any type of guarantee assurance. The trademarks that are used are without any consent, and the publication of the trademark is without permission or backing by the trademark owner. All trademarks and brands within this book are for clarifying purposes only and are the owned by the owners themselves, not affiliated with this document.

Table of Contents

Chapter 1

Understanding Customer-Centricity

What is Customer-Centricity?

Customer-centricity is an organizational approach that places the customer at the heart of all business decisions and operations. Unlike traditional business models that prioritize product development, sales targets, or profit margins, customer-centricity focuses on understanding and fulfilling customer needs and desires. This approach requires a deep commitment to listening to customers, understanding their pain points, and consistently delivering value in ways that foster loyalty and satisfaction.

At its core, customer-centricity involves a shift in mindset. It is not merely a strategy but a company-wide culture that prioritizes the customer's perspective. This means that every department, from marketing to product development to customer service, must work in harmony to create positive customer experiences. The ultimate goal is to build long-term relationships with customers, ensuring their needs are met at every interaction with the brand.

The evolution of customer expectations has played a significant role in the rise of customer-centricity. In the past, consumers had limited choices and often made purchasing decisions based on price and availability. However, the digital age has empowered customers with a wealth of information and options at their fingertips. Today's consumers expect personalized experiences, immediate responses, and seamless interactions across multiple channels. They are more informed and more demanding, and they are not afraid to switch brands if their expectations are not met.

Businesses that adopt a customer-centric approach can reap numerous benefits. Customer-centric companies often enjoy higher customer satisfaction rates, increased loyalty, and stronger brand advocacy. When customers feel valued and understood, they are more likely to return and recommend the brand to others. This loyalty translates into higher lifetime value and lower customer acquisition costs, as satisfied customers become brand ambassadors.

Moreover, customer-centricity can drive innovation. By focusing on customer needs and feedback, companies can identify gaps in the market and develop products or services that better serve their audience. This proactive approach to innovation ensures that companies stay relevant and competitive in a rapidly changing marketplace.

Despite its advantages, there are common misconceptions about what it means to be customer-centric. One such misconception is that customer-centricity is synonymous with customer service. While excellent customer service is a crucial component, it is only one aspect of a broader strategy. True customer-centricity involves every stage of the customer journey, from initial awareness to post-purchase support. It requires a holistic approach that integrates customer insights into all business functions.

Another misconception is that customer-centricity means always saying "yes" to the customer. While it is essential to listen and respond to customer needs, it is equally important to manage expectations and maintain a balance between customer demands and business objectives. Sometimes, saying "no" or offering an alternative solution is necessary to preserve the integrity of the brand and ensure long-term success.

To illustrate the impact of customer-centricity, consider the case of companies that have successfully adopted this approach. One notable example is Amazon. From its inception, Amazon has prioritized customer satisfaction, offering features like personalized recommendations, customer reviews, and a user-friendly interface. Their commitment to fast, reliable delivery through services like Amazon Prime has set a new standard for e-commerce. Amazon's relentless focus on the customer has driven its growth and established it as a leader in the retail industry.

Another example is Apple. Apple's success can be attributed to its deep understanding of its customers' desires for sleek, intuitive, and high-quality products. By consistently delivering products that exceed customer expectations and creating seamless experiences across their ecosystem, Apple has built a loyal customer base that eagerly anticipates each new product release. Their commitment to design and usability is a testament to their customer-centric philosophy.

Customer-centricity is not without its challenges. It requires significant investment in time, resources, and technology. Companies must be willing to invest in robust data analytics to gather and interpret customer insights. This data-driven approach allows businesses to tailor their offerings and communications to meet specific customer needs. Additionally, fostering a customer-centric culture involves training employees at all levels to prioritize customer satisfaction and align their actions with the company's customer-centric goals.

Leadership plays a crucial role in driving a customer-centric culture. Leaders must champion the cause, setting the tone from the top and demonstrating a genuine commitment to customer-centricity. This involves empowering employees to make decisions that benefit the customer, even if it means deviating from standard procedures. Leaders should also encourage cross-functional collaboration, ensuring that all departments work together to deliver a cohesive customer experience.

Employee engagement is another critical factor. When employees feel valued and understand their role in the customer journey, they are more likely to go above and beyond to meet customer needs. Providing training and development opportunities can help employees develop the skills necessary to deliver exceptional customer experiences. Recognizing and rewarding employees who exemplify customer-centric behaviors can further reinforce the importance of putting the customer first.

Technology is a vital enabler of customer-centricity. Advanced customer relationship management (CRM) systems allow companies to track customer interactions, preferences, and feedback in real-time. This information can be used to personalize communications, anticipate needs, and resolve issues promptly. Additionally, leveraging artificial intelligence and machine learning can enhance customer insights and automate processes, freeing up employees to focus on more value-added activities.

Despite the challenges, the rewards of a customer-centric approach are well worth the effort. Companies that successfully implement customer-centric strategies often see increased customer retention, higher revenue, and a stronger competitive position. By prioritizing the customer in every decision and action, businesses can create lasting value for both their customers and themselves.

In conclusion, customer-centricity is a transformative approach that requires a fundamental shift in how businesses operate. It demands a deep understanding of customer needs, a commitment to continuous improvement, and a willingness to invest in the necessary resources and technology. By placing the customer at the center of their universe, companies can build stronger relationships, drive innovation, and achieve sustainable growth in today's competitive landscape.

A key aspect of maintaining customer-centricity is the ongoing process of gathering and analyzing customer feedback. This feedback loop is essential for understanding how well the company is meeting customer expectations and identifying areas for improvement. Companies can use various methods to collect feedback, including surveys, interviews, focus groups, and social media monitoring. Each of these methods provides valuable insights that can help shape business strategies and enhance the customer experience.

The Evolution of Customer Expectations

Customer expectations have undergone a profound transformation over the years, driven by technological advancements, increased access to information, and a shift in the balance of power between businesses and consumers. Understanding this evolution is crucial for any company aiming to meet and exceed customer demands in today's competitive landscape.

In the early days of commerce, customer expectations were relatively straightforward. The primary concerns were product availability and price. Customers had limited choices and often depended on local merchants to meet their needs. Personal relationships between buyers and sellers played a significant role, with customer loyalty often based on trust and familiarity.

As industrialization took hold in the late 19th and early 20th centuries, mass production and distribution began to change the marketplace. Products became more standardized, and price competition increased. Customers started to expect consistent quality and value for money. The rise of department stores and mail-order catalogs expanded consumer choices and introduced the notion of convenience in shopping. Yet, customer expectations remained largely transactional.

The latter half of the 20th century saw the advent of modern marketing techniques. Companies began to understand the importance of branding and customer segmentation. Advertising became a powerful tool to shape customer perceptions and create demand. During this period, expectations shifted again, with customers seeking not just products, but also the lifestyle and status associated with certain brands. The emphasis was on differentiation and emotional appeal.

The digital revolution of the late 20th and early 21st centuries marked a significant turning point. The internet democratized information, empowering customers with unprecedented access to product details, reviews, and price comparisons. E-commerce introduced convenience at a new level, allowing customers to shop from anywhere at any time. This era saw the rise of customer-centric companies like Amazon, which set new standards for speed, reliability, and customer service. Expectations began to include not just the quality of the product, but the entire purchasing experience.

Today, customer expectations are more complex and demanding than ever. They are shaped by several key factors:

1. **Personalization**: Customers expect personalized experiences tailored to their individual preferences and behaviors. This includes personalized recommendations, targeted marketing, and customized products or services. Companies like Netflix and Spotify have set high standards by using sophisticated algorithms to deliver personalized content.

2. **Speed and Convenience**: The digital age has created an expectation for instant gratification. Customers expect fast, efficient service and immediate access to information. The success of companies like Uber and Door Dash, which offer on-demand services, exemplifies this trend. Customers are no longer willing to wait; they want everything now.

3. **Omni channel Experience**: Customers interact with brands across multiple channels—online, in-store, mobile, social media—and expect a seamless experience across all of them. Consistency and integration are key. For example, a customer should be able to start a purchase on a mobile app, continue it on a desktop, and complete it in-store without any friction.

4. **Transparency and Trust**: In an era of information overload, transparency has become crucial. Customers expect honesty and openness from brands. They want to know where products come from, how they are made, and that they can trust the company's claims. This is particularly important in sectors like

food, fashion, and technology, where ethical considerations and sustainability are increasingly important.

5. **Customer Support and Engagement**: Excellent customer support is no longer optional; it is a fundamental expectation. Customers expect quick and effective resolution of their issues, often through multiple channels such as phone, email, chat, and social media. Moreover, they seek proactive engagement, where companies anticipate their needs and address them even before they arise.

6. **Value Beyond the Product**: Customers are looking for brands that offer value beyond the product itself. This can be through educational content, community building, or social responsibility initiatives. Brands that contribute positively to society and create a sense of community around their products tend to build stronger loyalty.

Meeting these modern expectations requires a strategic approach. Companies must leverage data and technology to understand their customers deeply. This involves collecting and analyzing data from various touchpoints to gain insights into customer behavior and preferences. Advanced analytics and customer relationship management (CRM) systems are essential tools in this regard.

However, technology alone is not enough. A customer-centric culture is vital. All employees, from front-line staff to top executives, must be aligned with the company's commitment to customer satisfaction. Training programs, clear communication of customer-centric values, and empowering employees to make decisions in the best interest of the customer are crucial elements.

Innovation also plays a critical role. Companies must continuously seek new ways to enhance the customer experience. This could involve adopting new technologies, improving processes, or developing new products and services. Staying ahead of customer expectations requires a proactive approach to innovation.

Consider the example of a traditional retail company adapting to modern customer expectations. This company might start by developing an e-commerce platform to provide online shopping. It would use data analytics to personalize product recommendations and marketing messages. An omnichannel strategy would ensure that customers have a consistent experience whether they shop online, in-store, or through a mobile app. The company would invest in fast and reliable delivery options, perhaps even experimenting with same-day delivery. It would also ensure robust customer support across multiple channels and engage customers with content and initiatives that reflect its brand values.

The evolution of customer expectations is an ongoing process. As technology advances and societal values shift, customers will continue to raise the bar. Companies that succeed will be those that not only meet but anticipate these evolving expectations. They will be agile, innovative, and deeply committed to understanding and serving their customers.

In conclusion, the journey of customer expectations from simple product availability to the complex, personalized, and integrated experiences demanded today reflects broader changes in society, technology, and business practices. Companies must adapt to these changes by leveraging technology, fostering a customer-centric culture, and continuously innovating. By doing so, they can build lasting relationships with their customers and thrive in the competitive marketplace.

In navigating the evolution of customer expectations, companies must embrace a holistic approach that integrates various facets of the business, from marketing and sales to operations and customer service. The interconnectedness of these elements creates a cohesive and compelling customer experience that not only meets but exceeds expectations.

Benefits of a Customer-Centric Approach

Adopting a customer-centric approach can significantly transform a business, leading to numerous tangible and intangible benefits. This strategy, which places the customer at the heart of all decision-making processes, can drive growth, enhance brand loyalty, and create a sustainable competitive advantage. To truly understand the benefits, it is essential to delve into the various ways in which a customer-centric mindset impacts a business.

One of the most immediate benefits of a customer-centric approach is improved customer satisfaction. When a company prioritizes the needs and preferences of its customers, it creates products and services that resonate more deeply with them. This alignment between customer expectations and company offerings leads to higher satisfaction levels. Satisfied customers are more likely to become repeat buyers, recommend the brand to others, and leave positive reviews, all of which contribute to increased revenue and market share.

Consider the case of a small e-commerce business that listens carefully to its customers' feedback about product quality and delivery times. By addressing these concerns promptly, the business not only retains its existing customers but also attracts new ones through positive word-of-mouth. This virtuous cycle of satisfaction and loyalty underscores the direct correlation between a customer-centric approach and business success.

Another significant benefit is the enhancement of customer loyalty. Loyal customers are invaluable assets to any business. They tend to spend more over time and are less sensitive to price changes, providing a stable revenue stream. A customer-centric approach fosters loyalty by building trust and demonstrating that the company values its customers' input and strives to meet their needs. This trust is crucial in an era where consumers have countless alternatives and can easily switch brands.

A practical example of fostering loyalty can be seen in the practices of many subscription-based services. These companies often offer personalized experiences, such as tailored recommendations and exclusive content, to their subscribers. By making customers feel special and understood, these businesses create a strong emotional bond that translates into long-term loyalty and reduced churn rates.

Implementing a customer-centric strategy also leads to better product development. When businesses actively seek and incorporate customer feedback, they are more likely to create products that meet market demands. This proactive approach reduces the risk of product failures and ensures that new offerings are well-received. Furthermore, involving customers in the development process can lead to innovative ideas that the company might not have considered otherwise.

A notable example of this can be seen in the technology sector, where companies frequently release beta versions of their software to gather user feedback. This iterative process allows them to refine their products based on real-world usage, resulting in more robust and user-friendly final versions. By valuing customer input, these companies not only improve their products but also signal to their customers that their opinions matter.

Additionally, a customer-centric approach can enhance brand reputation. In today's digital age, where information travels quickly and broadly, maintaining a positive brand image is crucial. Companies that consistently demonstrate a commitment to their customers are viewed more favorably. This positive perception can be a significant differentiator in competitive markets. A strong reputation attracts not only customers but also top talent, investors, and partners, all of which contribute to a company's growth and success.

For instance, a company known for its exceptional customer service will likely enjoy a strong reputation that precedes it. Potential customers, having heard positive stories and testimonials, will be more inclined to choose this company over competitors. This reputational advantage is a powerful asset that enhances customer acquisition and retention.

From an internal perspective, a customer-centric approach can lead to a more motivated and engaged workforce. When employees see that their efforts directly contribute to customer satisfaction, they are more likely to feel a sense of purpose and fulfillment. This alignment between employee roles and customer outcomes fosters a positive work environment and can lead to higher levels of employee retention and productivity.

Consider a customer service team that receives regular feedback on how their interactions have positively impacted customers. This feedback can be incredibly motivating, reinforcing the importance of their work and encouraging them to continue delivering high-quality service. A motivated workforce, in turn, enhances the overall customer experience, creating a positive feedback loop.

Financially, a customer-centric approach can lead to cost savings. By focusing on customer retention and satisfaction, businesses can reduce the costs associated with acquiring new customers, which are typically higher than those of maintaining existing ones. Moreover, loyal customers are more likely to engage in repeat purchases and provide free word-of-mouth marketing, further reducing marketing and sales expenses.

A practical example of cost savings can be observed in the realm of customer support. Companies that invest in understanding their customers' needs and proactively addressing common issues often experience a reduction in support inquiries. This efficiency not only saves costs but also improves the customer experience, as issues are resolved more swiftly and effectively.

Lastly, a customer-centric approach promotes long-term sustainability. In a rapidly changing business environment, companies that remain attuned to their customers' evolving needs are better positioned to adapt and thrive. This adaptability is crucial for sustaining growth and remaining relevant in the face of new competitors, technological advancements, and shifting market dynamics.

Consider the retail industry, where customer preferences can change rapidly. Companies that continually engage with their customers and adjust their offerings accordingly are more likely to stay ahead of trends and maintain their market position. This foresight and responsiveness are key to long-term success.

In conclusion, the benefits of a customer-centric approach are manifold and far-reaching. From improved customer satisfaction and loyalty to enhanced product development and brand reputation, this strategy offers a comprehensive framework for business success. Internally, it leads to a more engaged workforce and operational efficiencies, while financially, it provides cost savings and sustainable growth. By placing the customer at the center of their operations, businesses can create a virtuous cycle of satisfaction, loyalty, and innovation that drives long-term success. This holistic approach not only meets but anticipates customer needs, ensuring that companies remain competitive and relevant in an ever-evolving marketplace.

Building on the transformative power of a customer-centric approach, businesses can also unlock new opportunities for personalized marketing. Personalization goes beyond merely addressing customers by their first names in emails; it involves delivering tailored experiences based on individual preferences, behaviors, and past interactions. This deep level of customization not only enhances the customer experience but also significantly boosts engagement and conversion rates.

Common Misconceptions

Common misconceptions can derail even the most well-intentioned efforts in any field. In business, these misunderstandings can lead to poor decisions, inefficiencies, and lost opportunities. Addressing and debunking these misconceptions is critical for anyone aiming to achieve success. Here are some of the most prevalent myths and the realities that dispel them.

One of the most pervasive misconceptions is that the customer is always right. While it's important to value customer feedback and strive to meet their needs, this belief can lead to unsustainable practices and unrealistic expectations. Not all customer demands are reasonable or beneficial to the business. For instance, if a customer insists on an impractical feature that would require significant resources but benefit only a few, it might not be a wise business decision to comply. Instead, businesses should aim for a balance, valuing customer input while making decisions that align with their strategic goals and resources.

Another common misconception is that high sales volume equates to high profitability. Many businesses fall into the trap of focusing solely on increasing sales without considering the associated costs. High sales do not necessarily mean high profits, especially if the cost of acquiring those sales is exorbitant. For example, aggressive discounting strategies might boost sales numbers but can erode profit margins and damage the brand's perceived value. It's essential to maintain a holistic view of the business, considering both revenue and expenses to ensure sustainable profitability.

Some believe that marketing is only about advertising. This narrow view overlooks the multifaceted nature of marketing, which encompasses everything from market research and product development to pricing strategies and customer service. Advertising is just one component of a comprehensive marketing strategy. Effective marketing involves understanding the market, identifying customer needs, and creating value propositions that resonate with the target audience. For instance, a company might invest in content marketing to educate and engage its audience or in improving customer experiences to foster loyalty, both of which are integral to successful marketing.

There's also the misconception that a great product will sell itself. While having a high-quality product is crucial, it's not enough on its own. Even the best products need strategic marketing to reach their target audience and communicate their value effectively. Consider the numerous innovative products that have failed because of poor marketing. A well-crafted marketing strategy that includes market analysis, effective communication, and robust distribution channels is necessary to ensure that a great product reaches its full potential.

Many businesses operate under the false assumption that all customers are equally valuable. In reality, customers vary widely in their profitability and strategic importance. Some customers may generate high revenue but also require significant resources and attention, while others may be low-maintenance but highly profitable. It's crucial to segment customers and tailor strategies accordingly. For instance, a business might focus on nurturing relationships with high-value customers through personalized services and loyalty programs, while employing more automated and cost-effective methods for lower-value segments.

Another damaging misconception is that business success is solely about making money. While profitability is essential, focusing only on financial metrics can lead to short-sighted decisions that harm the business in the long term. Sustainable success involves balancing financial goals with other factors such as customer satisfaction, employee engagement, and corporate social responsibility. Companies that prioritize these aspects often find that they enhance their financial performance as well. For example, businesses that invest in employee development and a positive workplace culture tend to enjoy higher productivity, lower turnover, and better customer service, all of which contribute to long-term profitability.

The belief that more features make a product better is another common fallacy. While adding features can enhance a product's appeal, it can also lead to complexity and diminished user experience. This phenomenon, known as feature creep, can overwhelm customers and make the product less intuitive. Instead of indiscriminately adding features, businesses should focus on identifying and implementing the features that provide the most value to their customers. For example, a software company might focus on refining its core functionalities to ensure they are robust and user-friendly rather than continually adding new, but potentially unnecessary, features.

There's also a tendency to underestimate the importance of company culture. Some believe that culture is a soft, intangible aspect of business that doesn't significantly impact performance. However, a strong, positive culture can be a critical differentiator in a competitive market. It influences employee satisfaction, retention, and productivity, which in turn affects customer satisfaction and overall business success. Companies with a well-defined culture that aligns with their values and mission are often more resilient and better positioned to achieve sustainable growth. For instance, a company that fosters a culture of innovation and collaboration is likely to be more agile and responsive to market changes.

Another misconception is that growth always requires significant investment. While scaling a business often involves increased spending, it's not the only path to growth. Businesses can achieve growth through improving efficiencies, leveraging existing resources more effectively, and pursuing strategic partnerships. For example, a company might focus on optimizing its supply chain to reduce costs and improve margins, or it could form alliances with complementary businesses to reach new markets without substantial capital investment.

Finally, many believe that business success relies solely on the efforts of top management. While leadership plays a crucial role, the contributions of all employees are vital to achieving business goals. Engaging and empowering employees at all levels can lead to more innovative ideas, better problem-solving, and a stronger commitment to the company's success. Businesses that foster an inclusive environment where employees feel valued and heard are often more dynamic and successful. For instance, frontline employees who interact with customers daily can provide valuable insights into customer needs and preferences, which can inform strategic decisions.

In summary, challenging and correcting these common misconceptions is essential for building a robust and adaptable business. By recognizing that the customer is not always right, understanding that high sales don't always equal high profits, appreciating the multifaceted nature of marketing, and acknowledging the importance of strategic customer segmentation, businesses can make more informed and effective decisions. Moreover, balancing financial goals with broader success metrics, focusing on user-centric product development, cultivating a strong company culture, exploring alternative growth strategies, and valuing the contributions of all employees are critical for sustainable success. By addressing these misconceptions, businesses can create a more realistic, balanced, and ultimately successful approach to achieving their goals.

One area where many businesses falter is in their understanding of innovation. The misconception that innovation is all about groundbreaking inventions or technological advancements can be incredibly limiting. True innovation involves a broader spectrum: it includes incremental improvements, process optimizations, and new business models that collectively drive progress. For instance, a company might innovate by refining its customer service processes, leading to greater efficiency and enhanced customer satisfaction, rather than focusing solely on launching a new product.

Case Studies of Customer-Centric Companies

Case studies of customer-centric companies offer valuable lessons for businesses aiming to prioritize their customers. These companies have not only succeeded in meeting customer needs but have also created exceptional experiences that foster loyalty and drive growth. By examining these examples, we can uncover practical strategies and insights that can be applied to any business.

One notable example is Amazon. From its inception, Amazon has placed a relentless focus on customer satisfaction. This commitment is evident in their customer service policies, user-friendly website, and innovative services like Amazon Prime. Amazon's recommendation engine, which suggests products based on customer behavior, exemplifies how data can be used to enhance the shopping experience. The company's dedication to fast, reliable delivery has set industry standards. By continually refining their logistics and fulfillment processes, Amazon ensures that customers receive their orders quickly and reliably, reinforcing trust and encouraging repeat business.

Zappos, an online shoe and clothing retailer, is another shining example of customer-centricity. Zappos' CEO, Tony Hsieh, famously prioritized customer service as the cornerstone of the company's culture. Employees are empowered to go above and beyond to make customers happy, sometimes even directing customers to competitors if Zappos doesn't have the desired product in stock. This level of service has built a loyal customer base that appreciates the company's transparency and dedication. Zappos' focus on creating a positive work environment also translates into better customer interactions, as happy employees are more likely to provide excellent service.

Apple Inc. has revolutionized customer experience in the technology sector. Apple stores are designed to be more than just retail spaces; they are experiences. The Genius Bar, where customers can receive technical support and personal training, is a testament to Apple's commitment to customer education and satisfaction. Apple's product design philosophy, which emphasizes simplicity and user-friendliness, makes technology accessible and enjoyable, fostering a strong emotional connection with the brand. The seamless integration of hardware, software, and services ensures that customers have a consistent and high-quality experience across all Apple products.

The Ritz-Carlton Hotel Company sets the gold standard for customer service in the hospitality industry. Their motto, "We are Ladies and Gentlemen serving Ladies and Gentlemen," reflects their commitment to treating both employees and guests with the utmost respect and care. The Ritz-Carlton empowers its employees to spend up to $2,000 per guest per incident to resolve any issues and enhance the guest experience. This level of autonomy ensures that problems can be addressed swiftly and satisfactorily. The company's meticulous attention to detail and personalized service create memorable experiences that keep guests returning.

Southwest Airlines is well-known for its customer-centric approach in an industry often criticized for poor service. Southwest has built a reputation for friendly, reliable service and a no-frills, no-fees approach that resonates with cost-conscious travelers. Their open seating policy, which eliminates assigned seats, speeds up boarding and allows for more flexibility. Southwest's culture, which emphasizes humor and a positive attitude, helps create a pleasant travel experience. Their transparency about fees and policies builds trust with customers, fostering loyalty even in a highly competitive market.

Trader Joe's, a popular grocery store chain, focuses on delivering exceptional value and a unique shopping experience. Trader Joe's carefully curates its product selection, offering high-quality items at competitive prices. Their stores are designed to be inviting and easy to navigate, with friendly employees known as "Crew Members" who provide personalized service and often go out of their way to assist customers. Trader Joe's also places a strong emphasis on creating a fun and engaging atmosphere, from their quirky product labels to their in-store tastings and demos.

Nordstrom, a luxury department store, is renowned for its exceptional customer service. Nordstrom's liberal return policy, which allows customers to return items without a receipt and with no time limit, exemplifies their commitment to customer satisfaction. Their sales associates are known for providing personalized service, often going to great lengths to ensure customers find exactly what they need. Nordstrom also leverages technology to enhance the shopping experience, offering services like curbside pickup and virtual styling appointments. This blend of high-touch service and technological convenience helps Nordstrom maintain a loyal customer base.

Disney is another iconic example of customer-centricity, especially within its theme parks and resorts. Disney's focus on creating magical experiences is embedded in every aspect of their operations, from the meticulously maintained parks to the friendly and helpful cast members. Disney uses sophisticated data analytics to understand guest preferences and improve their experience, whether through queue management systems that reduce wait times or personalized recommendations. The company's attention to detail and commitment to storytelling ensure that guests are fully immersed in the Disney experience, creating lasting memories and fostering brand loyalty.

Tesla, the electric vehicle manufacturer, has redefined the automotive industry with its customer-centric approach. Tesla's direct-to-consumer sales model allows for a more personalized buying experience, eliminating the traditional dealership model. Their over-the-air software updates ensure that customers' vehicles are continually improved, adding new features and enhancing performance without the need for a visit to a service center. Tesla's commitment to sustainability and innovation resonates strongly with its customer base, creating a community of loyal advocates for the brand.

Finally, Patagonia, the outdoor clothing and gear company, exemplifies how a strong commitment to social and environmental responsibility can drive customer loyalty. Patagonia's dedication to sustainability is evident in its products, which are designed to be durable and environmentally friendly. The company also encourages customers to repair and recycle their gear rather than buying new items, reinforcing their commitment to reducing waste. Patagonia's activism on environmental issues resonates with its customer base, creating a strong emotional connection and a sense of shared values.

These case studies demonstrate that a customer-centric approach can take many forms, from exceptional service and personalized experiences to innovative products and strong ethical commitments. What they all have in common is a deep understanding of their customers' needs and a relentless focus on meeting those needs in ways that create value and foster loyalty. By studying these examples, businesses can glean valuable insights and strategies that can be adapted to their own unique contexts, ultimately leading to greater customer satisfaction and long-term success.

While these companies operate in diverse industries, they share several key principles that drive their customer-centric success. First and foremost is a deep commitment to understanding their customers. This involves not just collecting data, but also actively listening to customer feedback and observing behaviors to gain insights into their needs and preferences. For instance, Amazon's use of customer reviews and shopping data allows them to continuously refine their product recommendations and improve the overall shopping experience.

Chapter 2

Knowing Your Customer

Market Research Techniques

Understanding your market is the cornerstone of any successful business strategy. Market research provides the insights needed to make informed decisions, identify opportunities, and mitigate risks. Various techniques can be employed to gather this critical information, each with its own strengths and applications.

Surveys are among the most common and versatile market research tools. They can be conducted online, over the phone, through email, or in person. Surveys allow businesses to collect quantitative data on customer preferences, behaviors, and opinions. Designing an effective survey involves crafting clear, concise questions that avoid bias and encourage honest responses. To ensure a representative sample, it's important to reach a diverse audience. Tools like Google Forms, SurveyMonkey, and Qualtrics can help streamline the survey process and analyze the results.

Focus groups offer a more qualitative approach, providing deeper insights into customer attitudes and perceptions. In a focus group, a small group of participants discusses a product, service, or concept under the guidance of a moderator. This setting allows for dynamic interaction and can uncover nuanced opinions and emotional responses that might not emerge in a survey. However, focus groups require careful planning and skilled moderation to avoid groupthink and ensure that all voices are heard.

Another powerful technique is the use of interviews. One-on-one interviews can be structured, semi-structured, or unstructured, depending on the depth and flexibility required. Structured interviews follow a predetermined set of questions, ensuring consistency across interviews and facilitating easier comparison of responses. Semi-structured interviews provide a framework of key questions but allow for exploration of interesting topics as they arise. Unstructured interviews are more conversational, offering the greatest flexibility but requiring strong interviewing skills to keep the discussion focused and productive.

Observational research involves watching and recording how customers interact with products or services in natural settings. This technique provides real-world insights into customer behavior and can reveal pain points or opportunities that customers themselves might not articulate. For instance, a retailer might observe how shoppers navigate a store, identify popular product placements, and note any areas where customers seem confused or frustrated. While observational research can be time-consuming and requires careful documentation, it often yields valuable, actionable insights.

Ethnographic research takes observational techniques a step further by immersing researchers in the daily lives of their subjects. This approach is particularly useful for understanding complex social and cultural dynamics that influence customer behavior. By living and working alongside customers, researchers can gain a holistic view of their experiences, needs, and challenges. Ethnographic research is intensive and can take weeks or even months, but the deep, contextual understanding it provides can be invaluable, especially for developing products or services that fit seamlessly into customers' lives.

Secondary research, or desk research, involves analyzing existing data from various sources such as industry reports, academic studies, government publications, and news articles. This technique is cost-effective and provides a broad overview of market trends, competitive landscapes, and regulatory environments. Secondary research is often used to complement primary research methods, providing context and background information that can inform and refine research questions and hypotheses.

A more contemporary approach to market research involves social media listening. By monitoring conversations on platforms like Twitter, Facebook, Instagram, and LinkedIn, businesses can gauge public sentiment, track emerging trends, and identify influencers. Social media listening tools like Hootsuite, Brandwatch, and Sprout Social can automate much of this process, providing real-time insights and analytics. This technique allows businesses to react quickly to changes in the market and engage with customers directly in their preferred digital environments.

Another innovative technique is the use of online communities and panels. These are groups of pre-recruited individuals who agree to participate in ongoing research activities. Online panels can provide quick feedback on new ideas, test marketing messages, or explore customer satisfaction. The key advantage of this method is the ability to gather longitudinal data, tracking changes in opinions and behaviors over time. Building and maintaining an engaged panel requires effort, but the continuous access to a willing audience can significantly speed up the research process.

Experimentation, such as A/B testing, is a practical way to test hypotheses in a controlled environment. By comparing two versions of a product, webpage, or marketing campaign, businesses can identify which performs better in terms of customer engagement, conversion rates, or other key metrics. A/B testing provides clear, actionable insights and is particularly useful in digital marketing. Tools like Optimizely, Google Optimize, and Unbounce can help set up and analyze experiments, ensuring that decisions are based on solid data rather than intuition.

Lastly, conjoint analysis is a sophisticated technique used to understand how customers value different attributes of a product or service. By presenting customers with a series of choices that involve trade-offs, businesses can determine the relative importance of various features and the optimal combination of attributes. This method is especially useful for product development and pricing strategies, as it reveals which features are most likely to drive purchase decisions and how much customers are willing to pay for them.

Incorporating these market research techniques involves a blend of art and science. It requires careful planning, execution, and analysis to ensure that the data collected is reliable and actionable. Businesses must be clear about their research objectives, choose the appropriate methods, and be prepared to iterate based on the findings. Combining multiple techniques can provide a more comprehensive view of the market, leveraging the strengths of each method to compensate for their individual limitations.

Effective market research not only informs strategic decisions but also fosters a deeper connection with customers. By understanding their needs, preferences, and behaviors, businesses can develop products and services that truly resonate with their target audience. This customer-centric approach is crucial for building brand loyalty, driving growth, and staying competitive in an ever-evolving market landscape.

In summary, mastering market research techniques is essential for any business seeking to thrive in today's competitive environment. Whether through surveys, focus groups, interviews, observational research, ethnography, secondary research, social media listening, online panels, experimentation, or conjoint analysis, the key is to gather meaningful insights that drive informed decision-making. By continually refining these techniques and staying attuned to market dynamics, businesses can ensure they remain responsive to their customers' evolving needs and preferences, positioning themselves for sustained success.

Market research is not a one-time activity but an ongoing process. As markets evolve and customer preferences shift, businesses must remain agile and adaptable, continuously updating their knowledge and strategies. This iterative nature of market research ensures that companies can anticipate changes, stay relevant, and capitalize on new opportunities as they arise.

Creating Customer Personas

Understanding your customers is essential for any successful business, and creating detailed customer personas is a powerful way to achieve this. Customer personas are semi-fictional representations of your ideal customers based on data and research. These personas help you understand your customers' needs, behaviors, and preferences, allowing you to tailor your marketing strategies, product development, and customer service efforts effectively.

The process of creating customer personas begins with gathering as much information as possible about your existing and potential customers. Start by analyzing your current customer base. Look at demographic data such as age, gender, income level, education, and geographic location. This information can be obtained from your sales records, customer relationship management (CRM) systems, and web analytics tools. Understanding these basic demographic factors provides a foundation for more in-depth persona development.

Next, delve into psychographic data, which includes your customers' interests, values, lifestyle choices, and personality traits. Psychographics help paint a more vivid picture of your customers, going beyond superficial characteristics to understand what motivates them. This information can be gathered through surveys, interviews, and social media analysis. For example, you might discover that a significant portion of your customers values sustainability and prefers eco-friendly products. Such insights are crucial for developing targeted marketing messages and product offerings.

Behavioral data is another critical component of customer personas. This includes information about how customers interact with your brand, such as their purchasing habits, preferred communication channels, and brand loyalty. Analyzing purchase history, website behavior, and customer feedback can reveal patterns in how different segments of your audience engage with your business. For example, you might find that younger customers prefer shopping online and engaging with your brand on social media, while older customers are more likely to visit physical stores and respond to email newsletters.

Once you have gathered and analyzed this data, it's time to start building your personas. Aim for a mix of qualitative and quantitative insights to create well-rounded representations. Begin by identifying your primary customer segments. These segments should be distinct groups of customers who share similar characteristics and behaviors. For each segment, create a detailed persona that includes a name, age, background, and descriptive narrative.

Let's consider an example. Suppose you run an online fitness apparel store. One of your primary customer segments might be young professionals who are passionate about fitness and lead busy lives. You could create a persona named "Fit Fiona," a 28-year-old marketing manager who works long hours but makes time for daily workouts. Fiona values high-quality, stylish workout clothes that can transition from the gym to casual outings. She prefers shopping online due to her hectic schedule and follows fitness influencers on Instagram for fashion inspiration.

In addition to demographic and psychographic details, include Fiona's goals, challenges, and pain points. For instance, Fiona's goal might be to maintain a healthy lifestyle despite her busy career, while her challenge could be finding gym apparel that is both functional and fashionable. By identifying these elements, you can better understand her needs and tailor your marketing messages to address her specific concerns.

Creating multiple personas is often necessary to cover the diversity within your customer base. Aim for three to five personas that represent your most significant customer segments. Each persona should be distinct and based on the data you've collected. Avoid creating too many personas, as this can dilute your focus and make it challenging to develop targeted strategies.

Once your personas are developed, integrate them into your business strategies. Use them to guide your marketing campaigns, product development, and customer service initiatives. For example, when planning a new marketing campaign, refer to your personas to ensure your messaging resonates with your target audience. If you're launching a new product, consider how it meets the needs and preferences of your personas. In customer service, train your team to recognize and respond to the unique concerns of different personas, providing a more personalized experience.

Regularly review and update your personas to keep them relevant. Customer preferences and behaviors can change over time, so it's essential to stay current with market trends and feedback. Set a schedule for revisiting your personas, such as annually or biannually, and make adjustments based on new data and insights.

Storytelling is a powerful technique for bringing your customer personas to life. Crafting narratives around your personas helps your team visualize and empathize with your customers. For example, you might create a day-in-the-life story for each persona, detailing their daily routines, interactions with your brand, and key decision-making moments. These stories can be shared across your organization to ensure everyone understands and connects with your target audience.

Engage your team in the persona creation process. Collaborate with colleagues from different departments, such as marketing, sales, and customer service, to gather diverse perspectives and insights. This collaborative approach ensures that your personas are comprehensive and reflect the collective knowledge of your team. It also fosters a sense of ownership and alignment around your customer-centric strategies.

Utilize visual aids to make your personas more engaging and memorable. Design persona profiles with photos, quotes, and key characteristics that capture the essence of each persona. These profiles can be displayed in your office, included in training materials, and referenced during strategy meetings. Visual personas help keep your customers top of mind and serve as constant reminders of who you are trying to reach and serve.

Finally, measure the impact of using customer personas in your business. Track key performance indicators (KPIs) such as customer satisfaction, engagement rates, and conversion rates to assess how well your persona-driven strategies are working. Collect feedback from your team on the usefulness of personas in their daily work and make improvements as necessary. By continuously evaluating and refining your personas, you ensure they remain valuable tools for driving customer-centric success.

Creating customer personas is a strategic process that requires a blend of data analysis, creative thinking, and collaboration. By developing detailed personas based on demographic, psychographic, and behavioral data, you gain deep insights into your customers' needs and preferences. Integrating these personas into your business strategies helps you create more targeted, effective marketing campaigns, develop products that resonate with your audience, and provide exceptional customer service. Regularly updating your personas and measuring their impact ensures they remain relevant and valuable tools for achieving customer-centric success.

In addition to leveraging customer personas for internal alignment and strategy development, they can also play a significant role in external communications and brand positioning. When your marketing messages are crafted with specific personas in mind, they resonate more deeply with your target audience, fostering a sense of connection and loyalty. For instance, if your persona "Fit Fiona" values sustainability, highlighting your brand's eco-friendly practices and products will likely capture her interest and support. Tailoring your content to address the specific needs and values of each persona ensures that your marketing efforts are both relevant and compelling.

Understanding Customer Journeys

Mapping the customer journey is a crucial step in understanding how your customers interact with your brand, from the moment they become aware of your product to the point of purchase and beyond. This understanding enables you to create seamless, positive experiences that encourage customer loyalty and drive business growth. The customer journey is divided into several stages: awareness, consideration, decision, and post-purchase. Each stage represents a different mindset and set of behaviors from your customers, and it's essential to address their needs at each point.

The journey begins with awareness. This is when a potential customer first encounters your brand. They might come across your product through various channels—an online ad, a blog post, a social media mention, or word-of-mouth from a friend. At this stage, the customer may not yet recognize they have a need or problem that your product can solve. Your goal is to capture their interest and make a strong first impression. Content marketing, social media campaigns, and search engine optimization (SEO) are powerful tools for building awareness. By creating engaging, informative content that addresses common pain points, you can attract potential customers and introduce them to your brand.

Once a customer is aware of your brand, they move into the consideration stage. Here, they recognize a need or problem and begin actively seeking solutions. They compare different products and services, read reviews, and gather information to make an informed decision. This stage is critical for building trust and demonstrating the value of your offering. Providing detailed product information, case studies, customer testimonials, and comparison guides can help customers evaluate their options. It's important to address their questions and concerns clearly and honestly, positioning your product as the best solution for their needs.

As customers progress to the decision stage, they are ready to make a purchase. At this point, they need reassurance and a smooth, frictionless buying experience. Simplify the purchase process by offering clear calls to action, easy navigation, and multiple payment options. Providing excellent customer service, such as live chat support, can help address any last-minute questions or issues. Additionally, offering incentives like discounts, free trials, or money-back guarantees can nudge hesitant customers toward completing their purchase.

The customer journey doesn't end with the purchase. The post-purchase stage is crucial for fostering long-term loyalty and encouraging repeat business. After making a purchase, customers expect ongoing support and communication. Follow up with a thank-you email, provide detailed instructions for using your product, and offer channels for feedback or support. This stage is also an opportunity to turn satisfied customers into brand advocates. Encourage them to leave reviews, share their experiences on social media, and refer friends and family. A loyalty program can further incentivize repeat purchases and strengthen your relationship with your customers.

Understanding the emotional journey customers experience at each stage is equally important. During the awareness stage, customers may feel curiosity or excitement as they discover new products. In the consideration stage, these emotions might shift to uncertainty or anxiety as they weigh their options. The decision stage often involves a mix of anticipation and hesitation, while the post-purchase stage can bring satisfaction or disappointment depending on their experience. By acknowledging and addressing these emotions, you can create a more empathetic and supportive customer journey.

To effectively map the customer journey, start by gathering data from various sources. Customer surveys, interviews, and feedback forms provide direct insights into their experiences and pain points. Analytics tools can track behavior on your website, revealing which pages customers visit, how long they stay, and where they drop off. Social media listening tools can highlight common questions and concerns customers express online. Combining these qualitative and quantitative data sources gives you a comprehensive view of the customer journey.

Visualizing the customer journey through a journey map can help you identify key touchpoints and areas for improvement. A journey map is a visual representation of the steps customers take when interacting with your brand. It includes their actions, emotions, and pain points at each stage. By mapping out the journey, you can pinpoint moments where customers may encounter obstacles or friction. For example, if you notice a high drop-off rate during the checkout process, it may indicate that the process is too complicated or that customers are experiencing technical issues. Identifying these pain points allows you to make targeted improvements to enhance the overall experience.

Collaboration across departments is essential for creating an effective customer journey map. Marketing, sales, customer service, and product development teams all interact with customers in different ways and can provide valuable perspectives. By working together, you can ensure that the journey map accurately reflects the customer experience and identify opportunities for cross-functional improvements. Regularly reviewing and updating the journey map helps keep it relevant and aligned with changing customer needs and behaviors.

Personalization is a powerful strategy for enhancing the customer journey. Customers expect tailored experiences that address their individual needs and preferences. Use the data you've gathered to segment your audience and create personalized content, offers, and communications. For example, if a customer frequently purchases running gear from your sports apparel store, sending them personalized recommendations for new running shoes or apparel can increase their engagement and likelihood of making a purchase. Personalized experiences demonstrate that you understand and value your customers, fostering deeper connections and loyalty.

Technology plays a significant role in optimizing the customer journey. Customer relationship management (CRM) systems, marketing automation platforms, and analytics tools provide the data and insights needed to understand and improve the customer experience. These technologies enable you to track customer interactions across multiple channels, automate personalized communications, and measure the effectiveness of your efforts. Investing in the right tools and technologies can streamline the process of mapping and enhancing the customer journey.

Finally, measuring the success of your customer journey initiatives is crucial for continuous improvement. Define key performance indicators (KPIs) that align with your business goals, such as customer satisfaction scores, conversion rates, and customer lifetime value. Regularly monitor these metrics to assess the impact of your efforts and identify areas for further optimization. Collecting and analyzing customer feedback also provides valuable insights into their experiences and satisfaction levels. By continuously measuring and refining the customer journey, you can create a dynamic, responsive approach that meets evolving customer needs and drives business success.

Understanding the customer journey is essential for creating seamless, positive experiences that build loyalty and drive growth. By mapping the journey from awareness to post-purchase, addressing emotional and practical needs at each stage, and leveraging data and technology, you can optimize every touchpoint. Collaboration across departments and personalization further enhance the journey, ensuring that customers feel understood and valued. Regularly measuring and refining your efforts ensures that your customer journey strategies remain effective and aligned with your business goals. This comprehensive approach to understanding and improving the customer journey ultimately leads to happier customers and sustained business success.

One often overlooked but pivotal aspect of understanding customer journeys is identifying and nurturing key moments of truth. These are critical touchpoints where customers form lasting impressions of your brand. They can make or break customer loyalty. For instance, an exceptional unboxing experience or a prompt, helpful response from customer service can leave a positive impact, whereas a delayed shipment or a confusing return process can tarnish your brand's reputation. Recognizing these moments and ensuring they exceed customer expectations can significantly enhance the overall journey.

Leveraging Customer Feedback

Customer feedback is an invaluable asset for any business. It offers direct insights into what customers think about your products and services, highlights areas for improvement, and identifies what you're doing well. Effectively leveraging this feedback can transform your business, leading to better products, enhanced customer satisfaction, and increased loyalty. The key is not just collecting feedback but using it strategically to drive meaningful change.

Consider the story of a small coffee shop that started receiving comments about the long wait times during peak hours. Instead of dismissing these complaints, the owner decided to investigate further. They installed a simple feedback box and encouraged customers to share their thoughts. The responses were enlightening. Customers loved the coffee but were frustrated by the wait. Armed with this information, the owner hired an additional barista during busy times and streamlined the ordering process. Over time, customer satisfaction improved, word-of-mouth referrals increased, and the coffee shop saw a significant boost in sales.

The first step in leveraging customer feedback is to make it easy for customers to share their thoughts. This can be achieved through various channels such as surveys, feedback forms, social media, and review sites. Each channel provides different insights and reaches different segments of your customer base. For instance, while older customers might prefer email surveys, younger customers might be more inclined to leave feedback on social media. By offering multiple avenues for feedback, you ensure that all customers have a voice.

Once you have collected feedback, the next step is to analyze it. This involves categorizing comments to identify common themes and recurring issues. For example, if multiple customers mention that your website is difficult to navigate, this is a clear indication of an area that needs improvement. Advanced analytical tools can assist in this process by sorting through large volumes of feedback and highlighting key trends. Sentiment analysis, which assesses the emotional tone of feedback, can also provide deeper insights into how customers feel about different aspects of your business.

It's crucial to prioritize the issues that have the most significant impact on customer satisfaction and business performance. Not all feedback requires immediate action, and some suggestions might not align with your business goals. Focus on changes that will deliver the greatest benefits. For instance, if customers frequently complain about poor customer service, investing in training for your staff can have a profound impact on overall satisfaction.

Acting on feedback demonstrates to customers that you value their opinions and are committed to improving their experience. Transparency is essential in this process. Communicate the changes you're making based on customer feedback and explain how these changes will benefit them. This can be done through email newsletters, social media updates, or blog posts. For example, if you've improved your website's navigation based on customer suggestions, a simple message highlighting the new features can show customers that their input has been heard and appreciated.

Engaging customers in the feedback process can also foster a sense of community and loyalty. Invite them to participate in beta tests for new products or services, or create a customer advisory board to provide ongoing input. These initiatives not only make customers feel valued but also provide you with continuous, real-time feedback. For instance, a software company might invite a group of customers to test a new feature before its official release. Their feedback can help identify any issues and refine the feature, ensuring a smoother launch.

Measuring the impact of changes made based on customer feedback is critical to understand their effectiveness. Track key performance indicators (KPIs) such as customer satisfaction scores, Net Promoter Scores (NPS), and customer retention rates before and after implementing changes. This data can provide valuable insights into whether your actions are yielding the desired results. For instance, if your NPS improves after enhancing customer service training, it's a clear sign that the changes are having a positive impact.

Building a culture of continuous improvement within your organization is essential for effectively leveraging customer feedback. Encourage all employees to view feedback as an opportunity for growth rather than criticism. Regularly share customer feedback and the actions taken in response with your team. Recognize and reward employees who contribute to positive changes based on feedback. For example, a retail store might hold monthly meetings to review customer feedback and discuss potential improvements. Employees who receive positive mentions in feedback could be acknowledged for their exceptional service.

Technology can play a significant role in managing and leveraging customer feedback. Customer relationship management (CRM) systems, feedback management tools, and analytics platforms can streamline the collection, analysis, and action on feedback. These tools can help you organize feedback, identify trends, and track the impact of changes over time. For example, a CRM system can integrate feedback from various channels, providing a comprehensive view of customer sentiments and enabling more informed decision-making.

However, while technology is a powerful enabler, the human element remains crucial. Personal interactions and genuine responses to feedback can significantly enhance customer relationships. When customers see that their feedback is being addressed by real people who care about their experience, it fosters trust and loyalty. For example, a personalized thank-you note from a company's CEO addressing a customer's feedback can leave a lasting positive impression.

It's also important to recognize that feedback is a two-way street. While it's essential to listen to your customers, there are times when you need to educate them as well. For instance, if customers frequently misunderstand how to use a particular feature of your product, it might indicate a need for better instructional content or customer support. Providing clear, accessible resources can help customers get the most out of your product and reduce frustration.

Incorporating regular feedback loops into your product development cycle can lead to more customer-centric innovations. By involving customers early in the development process, you can ensure that new products and features align with their needs and preferences. For example, a tech company might conduct focus groups or surveys during the development of a new app to gather input on features and usability. This approach not only leads to better products but also builds anticipation and excitement among customers.

Lastly, consider the broader impact of customer feedback on your brand's reputation. Positive feedback can be a powerful marketing tool. Sharing customer success stories, testimonials, and positive reviews on your website and social media can enhance your brand's credibility and attract new customers. Conversely, how you handle negative feedback can also influence your reputation. Addressing issues promptly and professionally shows that you are committed to customer satisfaction and can turn a dissatisfied customer into a loyal advocate.

Leveraging customer feedback effectively requires a strategic approach that involves collecting, analyzing, prioritizing, and acting on feedback. It's about creating a culture of continuous improvement, engaging with customers, and using technology to support these efforts. By doing so, you can enhance customer satisfaction, drive business growth, and build a loyal customer base that advocates for your brand. The journey of leveraging customer feedback is ongoing, but the rewards are well worth the effort.

To truly harness the power of customer feedback, it's essential to foster an environment where feedback is not only welcomed but actively sought out. This means creating a culture within your organization that values customer insights and views them as integral to business success. From top management to frontline employees, everyone should understand the importance of customer feedback and their role in responding to it.

Analyzing Customer Data

Analyzing customer data is a critical component of modern business strategy. It transforms raw information into actionable insights, guiding decision-making and driving growth. Understanding how to effectively analyze customer data can help businesses optimize their operations, improve customer satisfaction, and gain a competitive edge. This chapter delves into the practical steps and methods for analyzing customer data, ensuring that even beginners can grasp the concepts and apply them effectively.

Imagine a retail store that collects data from various sources — point-of-sale systems, online purchases, loyalty programs, and customer surveys. This data, in its raw form, might seem overwhelming. However, with the right approach, it can reveal patterns and trends that are invaluable for business strategy. For instance, by analyzing purchase history, the store might identify that certain products sell best during specific seasons or that a particular demographic is more likely to buy high-margin items. Such insights can inform inventory management, marketing campaigns, and even store layout.

The first step in analyzing customer data is to collect it systematically. Data can come from multiple sources, including transaction records, social media interactions, customer service logs, and web analytics. It's essential to ensure that the data collected is accurate and comprehensive. For example, an e-commerce business might use cookies to track user behavior on their website, capturing data on pages visited, items viewed, and time spent on each page. This data provides a detailed picture of customer preferences and behavior.

Once data is collected, it needs to be cleaned and preprocessed. Data cleaning involves removing duplicates, correcting errors, and handling missing values. This step is crucial because inaccurate or incomplete data can lead to incorrect conclusions. For instance, if a customer survey contains multiple entries from the same individual, it can skew the results. Preprocessing might also involve standardizing data formats, such as ensuring that dates are consistently formatted or that product names are uniformly recorded.

With clean data, the next phase is to explore and visualize it. Exploratory data analysis (EDA) helps in understanding the basic structure and main characteristics of the data. Visualization tools such as charts, graphs, and heatmaps can highlight trends and patterns that might not be immediately obvious from raw numbers. For example, a heatmap of sales data might reveal that certain products perform exceptionally well in specific geographic regions. Visualization not only makes data more accessible but also aids in communicating findings to stakeholders who might not be as versed in data analysis.

Statistical analysis is another powerful tool in the data analyst's arsenal. Descriptive statistics, such as mean, median, and mode, provide a summary of the data. Inferential statistics, on the other hand, allow businesses to make predictions and generalizations about a population based on a sample. For instance, a company might use regression analysis to predict future sales based on historical data and external factors like economic trends. Hypothesis testing can determine if observed patterns are statistically significant or if they occurred by chance.

Segmentation is a technique that divides a customer base into distinct groups based on shared characteristics. This can be demographic information, purchasing behavior, or even response to marketing campaigns. By segmenting customers, businesses can tailor their strategies to meet the specific needs of different groups. For example, a travel agency might segment its customers into adventure seekers, luxury travelers, and budget-conscious tourists. Each segment can then receive personalized offers and communications that are more likely to resonate with them.

Predictive analytics takes data analysis a step further by using historical data to predict future outcomes.

Techniques such as machine learning and data mining can uncover patterns and relationships within the data that traditional methods might miss. For instance, a subscription service might use predictive analytics to anticipate which customers are likely to churn and proactively offer them incentives to stay. Similarly, analyzing past purchase behavior can help in forecasting demand for products, enabling better inventory management and reducing the risk of stockouts or overstocking.

A practical aspect of customer data analysis is the implementation of customer relationship management (CRM) systems. These systems consolidate customer information from various touchpoints, providing a unified view of each customer. CRM systems facilitate data analysis by making it easier to track interactions, manage customer profiles, and segment the customer base. For example, a CRM system can help a sales team identify high-value customers and prioritize their efforts accordingly, or allow a marketing team to design targeted campaigns based on detailed customer insights.

Another important consideration is the ethical use of customer data. Businesses must ensure they comply with data protection regulations, such as the General Data Protection Regulation (GDPR) in Europe and the California Consumer Privacy Act (CCPA) in the United States. This involves obtaining explicit consent from customers to collect and use their data, ensuring data security, and allowing customers to access and delete their information. Ethical data practices not only protect businesses from legal repercussions but also build trust with customers.

Data storytelling is a vital skill for effectively communicating insights derived from customer data. This involves crafting a narrative that explains the data's significance and implications in a clear and engaging manner. For instance, instead of just presenting statistics about declining customer satisfaction, a data story might include visualizations that show the trend over time, identify key factors contributing to the decline, and propose actionable solutions. Effective data storytelling helps ensure that insights lead to informed decision-making and tangible business outcomes.

Finally, continuous improvement is key to effective customer data analysis. The business environment and customer preferences are constantly evolving, so it's important to regularly update data collection methods, analysis techniques, and business strategies. This might involve adopting new technologies, training employees in advanced data analysis skills, or periodically reviewing key performance indicators to ensure they remain relevant. For example, as new social media platforms emerge, businesses might need to start collecting and analyzing data from these sources to stay attuned to their customers' changing behaviors and preferences.

In conclusion, analyzing customer data involves a systematic process of collecting, cleaning, exploring, and interpreting data to gain actionable insights. This process enables businesses to understand their customers better, predict future behaviors, and make informed decisions that drive growth. By prioritizing data accuracy, employing advanced analytical techniques, and continuously adapting to changes, businesses can leverage customer data to achieve a competitive advantage and foster lasting customer relationships. An often overlooked aspect of customer data analysis is the integration of qualitative data alongside quantitative data. While quantitative data provides measurable and statistical insights, qualitative data, such as customer reviews, feedback forms, and social media comments, offers context and depth. Combining these two types of data can provide a more comprehensive understanding of customer experiences and sentiments. For instance, analyzing customer reviews can reveal recurring themes about product issues or service gaps that might not be evident from numerical data alone. This can lead to more nuanced and effective improvements in products and services.

Chapter 3
Creating a Customer-Centric Culture

Leadership and Vision

Leadership and vision are the twin pillars upon which successful organizations are built. Effective leadership provides the direction and motivation needed to achieve goals, while a compelling vision offers a clear picture of the future that inspires and aligns the efforts of the entire team. These elements are inseparable and mutually reinforcing, creating a powerful synergy that drives organizational success.

Consider the story of Steve Jobs and Apple. Jobs was not just a leader; he was a visionary who saw beyond the immediate demands of the market to the future of technology. His vision for Apple wasn't merely about selling computers; it was about creating a seamless digital ecosystem that would transform how people interact with technology. This vision, paired with his relentless leadership, propelled Apple to unprecedented heights. Jobs's ability to articulate a clear and compelling vision, and then lead his team towards realizing that vision, exemplifies the profound impact of effective leadership and vision.

At its core, leadership is about influence. A great leader influences others to achieve a common goal, often by setting an example and demonstrating the behaviors and attitudes they wish to see in their team. This influence is rooted in trust, respect, and a shared commitment to the organization's vision. Leaders must possess a deep understanding of their values and beliefs, as these guide their decisions and actions. When leaders are clear about what they stand for, they can inspire others to follow them, fostering a sense of purpose and unity.

Vision, on the other hand, is the destination. It is the aspirational picture of what the organization aims to achieve in the future. A compelling vision provides direction and serves as a guiding star for strategic planning and decision-making. It helps the organization stay focused on long-term goals, even amid short-term challenges and setbacks. Crafting a vision requires foresight, creativity, and a deep understanding of the industry and market trends. It involves identifying opportunities and challenges, and imagining a future where the organization not only thrives but also makes a significant impact.

One of the key responsibilities of a leader is to communicate the vision effectively. This involves more than just sharing a statement; it requires telling a story that resonates with the team and stakeholders. The vision must be communicated in a way that is clear, compelling, and relatable. Leaders should use a variety of communication channels and methods to ensure that the vision is consistently reinforced. This could include speeches, meetings, written communications, and even informal conversations. The goal is to create a shared understanding and commitment to the vision, so that everyone in the organization is aligned and motivated to work towards it.

A great example of effective vision communication is Martin Luther King Jr.'s "I Have a Dream" speech. King painted a vivid and inspiring picture of a future where racial equality was a reality. His words galvanized a movement and mobilized countless individuals to take action. Similarly, organizational leaders must craft and communicate a vision that captures the imagination and passion of their team, encouraging them to contribute their best efforts towards achieving it.

Leadership also involves fostering a culture that supports the vision. This means creating an environment where the values and behaviors needed to achieve the vision are encouraged and rewarded. Leaders must be role models, demonstrating the commitment, integrity, and perseverance required to pursue the vision. They should also empower their team members, providing them with the resources, support, and autonomy needed to innovate and excel. By building a culture of trust, collaboration, and continuous improvement, leaders can ensure that their organization is well-equipped to navigate the journey towards its vision.

Moreover, effective leaders recognize the importance of adaptability and resilience. The path to realizing a vision is rarely linear; it is often fraught with obstacles and unforeseen challenges. Leaders must be willing to adapt their strategies and approaches in response to changing circumstances, while remaining steadfast in their commitment to the vision. This requires a balance of flexibility and determination, as well as the ability to learn from failures and setbacks. By fostering a growth mindset and encouraging their team to embrace challenges as opportunities for learning and development, leaders can maintain momentum and keep the organization moving forward.

In addition to internal leadership, external leadership is crucial for aligning the organization's vision with broader societal and market trends. This involves engaging with stakeholders, including customers, partners, and the community, to understand their needs and expectations. Leaders must be proactive in seeking feedback and building relationships that support the organization's vision. For instance, a company committed to sustainability might engage with environmental groups, policymakers, and consumers to promote and advance its sustainability initiatives. By aligning the vision with external trends and expectations, leaders can enhance the organization's reputation, credibility, and impact.

One practical approach to embedding vision into the fabric of an organization is through strategic planning. This process involves setting long-term goals that are aligned with the vision, and developing detailed plans to achieve these goals. Strategic planning should be an inclusive process, involving input from various levels of the organization to ensure that the plans are realistic and actionable. Leaders should regularly review and update the strategic plan to reflect progress and changes in the internal and external environment. By aligning daily operations and decisions with the long-term vision, strategic planning helps keep the organization focused and on track.

Furthermore, measurement and accountability are essential components of effective leadership and vision. Leaders must establish clear metrics and key performance indicators (KPIs) to track progress towards the vision. These metrics should be communicated transparently, and performance should be regularly reviewed and discussed. Accountability mechanisms, such as performance reviews and feedback systems, ensure that everyone in the organization is responsible for contributing to the vision. Recognizing and celebrating achievements, both big and small, can reinforce commitment and motivation.

Consider the case of Tesla and its CEO, Elon Musk. Musk's vision of accelerating the world's transition to sustainable energy has been a driving force behind Tesla's innovations in electric vehicles and renewable energy. Musk's leadership style, characterized by bold decision-making and a relentless focus on the vision, has inspired Tesla's team and captured the public's imagination. Despite numerous challenges and setbacks, Tesla has made significant strides towards its vision, illustrating the power of strong leadership and a compelling vision.

Leadership and vision are not static; they evolve over time. As the organization grows and the external environment changes, leaders must continuously refine and adapt their vision. This requires staying informed about industry trends, technological advancements, and shifts in customer preferences. Leaders should be open to new ideas and perspectives, and willing to pivot when necessary to ensure that the vision remains relevant and achievable. By maintaining a forward-looking perspective and fostering a culture of innovation, leaders can ensure that their organization remains agile and resilient in the face of change.

In conclusion, leadership and vision are critical components of organizational success. A visionary leader provides the direction and inspiration needed to achieve long-term goals, while effective leadership ensures that the organization remains aligned and motivated on the journey towards the vision. By communicating the vision clearly, fostering a supportive culture, adapting to challenges, and engaging with stakeholders, leaders can create a powerful and enduring impact. The synergy between leadership and vision drives innovation, growth, and lasting success, enabling organizations to navigate the complexities of the modern business landscape and achieve their full potential. Leadership and vision also require a commitment to ethical standards and social responsibility. Leaders must ensure that their vision aligns with ethical principles and contributes positively to society. This involves making decisions that are not only beneficial for the organization but also for the wider community and environment. Ethical leadership fosters trust and respect, both internally among employees and externally with customers, partners, and society at large. When leaders prioritize ethical behavior and social responsibility, they create a strong foundation for sustainable success.

Employee Engagement and Training

Employee engagement and training are crucial elements that drive an organization's success. Engaged employees are more productive, innovative, and committed to their work, while effective training ensures they have the necessary skills and knowledge to perform their roles efficiently. The synergy between engagement and training creates a dynamic and empowered workforce capable of achieving exceptional results.

Employee engagement begins with understanding what motivates and inspires individuals within the organization. It's about creating a workplace where employees feel valued, respected, and connected to the company's mission and values. This sense of belonging and purpose is a powerful driver of engagement, fostering a culture where employees are willing to go above and beyond in their roles.

One practical approach to enhancing employee engagement is through regular and meaningful communication. Leaders should make it a priority to communicate openly and transparently with their teams. This includes sharing organizational goals, updates, and challenges, as well as actively seeking feedback and input from employees. When employees feel informed and heard, they are more likely to feel invested in the success of the organization.

Consider the example of a tech startup that experienced rapid growth. The CEO recognized that maintaining high levels of engagement was critical to sustaining this momentum. To achieve this, the company implemented regular town hall meetings where leaders shared updates and successes, as well as addressing any concerns raised by employees. This open dialogue not only kept everyone informed but also fostered a sense of community and shared purpose.

Another key factor in employee engagement is recognition and appreciation. Employees need to know that their efforts are noticed and valued. This can be achieved through both formal recognition programs, such as employee of the month awards, and informal gestures, like a simple thank you note or public acknowledgment of a job well done. By celebrating achievements and milestones, leaders can reinforce positive behaviors and motivate employees to continue striving for excellence.

In addition to recognition, providing opportunities for growth and development is essential for keeping employees engaged. This is where training plays a pivotal role. Effective training programs equip employees with the skills and knowledge they need to perform their current roles and prepare them for future opportunities within the organization. This investment in employee development not only enhances performance but also demonstrates a commitment to their career progression.

Training should be tailored to meet the diverse needs and learning styles of employees. This might include a mix of on-the-job training, workshops, e-learning modules, and mentoring programs. For example, a manufacturing company might offer hands-on training for new equipment, while also providing online courses on industry best practices and safety protocols. By offering a variety of training options, organizations can ensure that all employees have access to the resources they need to succeed.

Leadership development is another critical aspect of training that can have a significant impact on employee engagement. Effective leaders are essential for creating a positive work environment and fostering a culture of engagement. Organizations should invest in leadership training programs that equip managers with the skills to lead, motivate, and support their teams. This might include training on communication, conflict resolution, and performance management.

Consider the case of a retail chain that faced high turnover rates among its store managers. To address this, the company implemented a comprehensive leadership development program that included workshops, coaching, and peer mentoring. The program not only improved the skills of existing managers but also created a pipeline of future leaders. As a result, turnover rates decreased, and employee engagement scores improved significantly.

While training is essential, it must be continuous and adaptable to changing needs and circumstances. The business landscape is constantly evolving, and organizations must ensure that their training programs keep pace with these changes. This requires regular assessment of training needs, as well as ongoing evaluation of training effectiveness. By staying agile and responsive, organizations can ensure that their workforce remains skilled and engaged in the face of new challenges and opportunities.

Moreover, integrating technology into training and engagement initiatives can enhance their effectiveness. Digital platforms can facilitate access to training materials, enable virtual collaboration, and provide real-time feedback. For instance, a global consulting firm might use an online learning management system to deliver training courses to employees in different locations, ensuring consistency and accessibility. Additionally, social media and collaboration tools can foster a sense of community and engagement among remote or dispersed teams.

Creating a culture of continuous learning and improvement is also vital for sustaining employee engagement. This involves encouraging employees to take ownership of their development and providing them with the resources and support they need to pursue new skills and knowledge. Organizations can promote a learning culture by offering incentives for continuous education, such as tuition reimbursement, and by recognizing and rewarding employees who demonstrate a commitment to their professional growth.

Consider the story of a healthcare organization that prioritized continuous learning. They implemented a program that provided financial support for employees seeking advanced certifications and degrees. Additionally, they created a library of online resources and encouraged employees to share their learning experiences through internal forums and workshops. This commitment to learning not only enhanced the skills of their workforce but also created a culture of engagement and collaboration.

Employee engagement and training are not just HR functions; they are strategic imperatives that require the involvement and commitment of leadership at all levels. Leaders must model the behaviors they wish to see, demonstrating a commitment to engagement and development through their actions and decisions. This might involve participating in training programs themselves, providing regular feedback and coaching, and creating opportunities for team-building and collaboration.

In conclusion, employee engagement and training are critical drivers of organizational success. Engaged employees are more productive, innovative, and committed, while effective training ensures they have the skills and knowledge needed to excel. By fostering a culture of open communication, recognition, growth, and continuous learning, organizations can create a dynamic and empowered workforce. Leaders play a vital role in this process, modeling the behaviors and values that drive engagement and development. Through strategic investment in engagement and training, organizations can achieve exceptional results and build a foundation for long-term success. One can observe the lasting impact of these principles in various organizations that have committed to fostering engagement and continuous development. Take, for example, a global financial services firm that faced the challenge of maintaining high engagement levels across its diverse and dispersed workforce. The firm introduced a comprehensive engagement strategy that included regular pulse surveys to gather employee feedback, a robust recognition program, and a strong emphasis on professional development.

Fostering a Customer-First Mindset

A customer-first mindset is the cornerstone of any successful business. It involves putting the needs and satisfaction of customers at the forefront of all business decisions and actions. Companies that embrace this approach often see increased customer loyalty, higher sales, and a stronger brand reputation. Developing a customer-first mindset starts with understanding who your customers are, what they need, and how your products or services can best meet those needs.

One of the most effective ways to understand your customers is through active listening. This means not just hearing what customers say, but truly understanding their concerns, preferences, and expectations. Consider the case of a small boutique that faced declining sales. The owner decided to hold a series of focus groups with regular customers to gather honest feedback. Through these discussions, she learned that customers wanted a more personalized shopping experience and a wider range of product options. By implementing these changes, sales began to improve, demonstrating the power of listening to customer feedback.

Incorporating customer feedback into business strategies is essential for fostering a customer-first mindset. This feedback can come from various sources, including surveys, social media, customer service interactions, and direct conversations. For example, an online retailer might use customer survey data to identify trends in product satisfaction and areas for improvement. By acting on this data, the retailer can make informed decisions that enhance the customer experience.

Another critical aspect of a customer-first mindset is empathy. Empathy involves putting yourself in the customer's shoes and understanding their emotions, challenges, and desires. This approach can transform how businesses interact with customers and address their needs. Imagine a software company that receives a complaint from a frustrated user struggling to navigate its platform. Instead of merely providing a technical solution, the customer support team takes the time to understand the user's frustration and offers additional guidance and resources. This empathetic approach not only resolves the issue but also strengthens the customer's trust and loyalty.

Building strong relationships with customers requires consistent and positive interactions across all touchpoints. Every interaction, whether it's a marketing email, a social media post, or a phone call with customer service, should reflect the company's commitment to customer satisfaction. A telecommunications company that struggled with negative customer perceptions decided to overhaul its customer service approach. They trained their representatives to not only resolve issues but also engage with customers in a friendly and supportive manner. Over time, this shift led to higher customer satisfaction scores and a more positive brand image.

Transparency and honesty are also vital components of a customer-first mindset. Customers appreciate businesses that are open about their processes, policies, and any issues that may arise. For instance, a food delivery service that encounters a delay in fulfilling an order should proactively inform the customer, explain the reason for the delay, and offer a gesture of goodwill, such as a discount on the next order. This level of transparency can turn a potentially negative experience into an opportunity to build trust and demonstrate commitment to customer care.

Empowering employees to make decisions that benefit customers is crucial for fostering a customer-first culture. Employees who feel trusted and valued are more likely to go the extra mile to ensure customer satisfaction. Consider a hotel chain that empowers its front-line staff to resolve guest complaints without needing managerial approval. This not only speeds up the resolution process but also shows guests that the hotel is dedicated to their comfort and satisfaction.

Training and development programs can play a significant role in instilling a customer-first mindset in employees. These programs should focus on customer service skills, empathy, communication, and problem-solving. For example, a retail company might implement a training program that includes role-playing exercises where employees practice handling various customer scenarios. By preparing employees to respond effectively to customer needs, the company enhances its overall customer service quality.

Creating a seamless and enjoyable customer experience requires attention to detail at every stage of the customer journey. From the moment a customer first learns about your brand to the post-purchase follow-up, each interaction should be designed with the customer's needs in mind. A well-known e-commerce platform excels in this area by offering an intuitive website, easy checkout process, and prompt customer support. These efforts ensure that customers have a positive experience every time they interact with the brand.

A customer-first mindset also involves continuously innovating and improving to meet evolving customer expectations. This means staying attuned to market trends, technological advancements, and customer feedback to identify opportunities for enhancement. A car manufacturer that consistently seeks customer input on new models and features can better align its products with customer preferences, ultimately driving higher sales and satisfaction.

Moreover, personalizing the customer experience can significantly enhance satisfaction and loyalty. Personalization involves tailoring interactions and offerings to individual customer preferences and behaviors. A streaming service that uses data analytics to recommend shows based on a user's viewing history provides a more engaging and relevant experience. This level of personalization makes customers feel valued and understood, reinforcing their connection to the brand.

Building a customer-first mindset extends beyond direct customer interactions; it should permeate the entire organizational culture. Leadership must model customer-centric behaviors and prioritize customer satisfaction in strategic decisions. This top-down approach ensures that every department, from product development to marketing to finance, aligns with the goal of delivering exceptional customer experiences.

Consider the story of a multinational consumer goods company that underwent a cultural transformation to become more customer-focused. The CEO led by example, regularly engaging with customers and emphasizing the importance of customer satisfaction in company meetings. This shift in culture required time and effort but eventually led to a more cohesive and customer-oriented organization.

Finally, measuring and analyzing customer satisfaction is essential for understanding the effectiveness of your customer-first initiatives. Key performance indicators (KPIs) such as Net Promoter Score (NPS), customer satisfaction scores (CSAT), and customer retention rates provide valuable insights into how well your company is meeting customer needs. Regularly reviewing these metrics helps identify areas for improvement and track progress over time.

For example, a financial services firm that tracks NPS can quickly identify changes in customer sentiment and respond accordingly. If the NPS drops, the firm can investigate the root causes and implement corrective actions to address customer concerns. This proactive approach demonstrates a commitment to continuous improvement and customer satisfaction.

In conclusion, fostering a customer-first mindset requires a comprehensive and sustained effort across all levels of an organization. By actively listening to customers, demonstrating empathy, building strong relationships, ensuring transparency, empowering employees, and continuously innovating, businesses can create a culture that prioritizes customer satisfaction. This mindset not only drives higher customer loyalty and retention but also contributes to long-term business success. Through strategic commitment and consistent execution, companies can build lasting and meaningful connections with their customers, ultimately achieving a competitive edge in the marketplace. The journey toward embedding a customer-first mindset is not without its challenges. It demands a shift in perspective, a willingness to adapt, and a commitment to placing the customer at the center of all business activities. Despite the complexities, the rewards are substantial, leading to a more resilient and competitive business.

Aligning Departments and Teams

Effective alignment of departments and teams is crucial for any organization's success. When all parts of a company work in harmony, it results in a cohesive strategy, streamlined processes, and a unified effort toward common goals. Misalignment, on the other hand, can lead to inefficiencies, misunderstandings, and missed opportunities. Aligning departments and teams requires clear communication, strategic planning, and a culture of collaboration.

The first step in aligning departments is to establish a clear and compelling vision for the organization. This vision should articulate the company's long-term goals and values, providing a shared sense of purpose. When team members understand how their work contributes to the broader objectives, they are more likely to work together effectively. For instance, a healthcare company might set a vision of improving patient outcomes through innovative treatments and compassionate care. By communicating this vision consistently, leaders can ensure that all departments, from research and development to patient services, are aligned in their efforts.

Clear communication channels are essential for alignment. This involves regular and transparent sharing of information across all levels of the organization. Leadership should provide updates on company progress, changes in strategy, and important decisions. Additionally, departments should be encouraged to share their goals, challenges, and achievements with each other. Consider the example of a technology firm that holds monthly town hall meetings where executives discuss company performance and answer employee questions. This open communication fosters a sense of inclusion and ensures that everyone is on the same page.

Collaboration tools and platforms can also play a significant role in enhancing communication and alignment. Tools like project management software, shared calendars, and instant messaging apps help teams stay connected and coordinate their efforts. For example, a marketing team using a project management platform can easily collaborate with the sales team on campaign strategies, track progress, and ensure that both departments are working toward the same objectives.

Developing cross-functional teams is another effective strategy for aligning departments. These teams, composed of members from different departments, work together on specific projects or initiatives. This approach not only brings diverse perspectives and skills to the table but also fosters a culture of collaboration and mutual respect. For instance, a retail company might create a cross-functional team to launch a new product line, including members from product development, marketing, finance, and customer service. By working together, they can ensure that the product launch is well-coordinated and meets the company's overall goals.

Leadership plays a critical role in promoting alignment. Leaders must model collaborative behavior and break down silos within the organization. This can be achieved by encouraging open dialogue, recognizing and rewarding collaborative efforts, and fostering an environment where teamwork is valued. For example, a CEO who regularly collaborates with different departments and highlights successful cross-departmental projects in company meetings sets a positive example for the rest of the organization.

Setting clear and aligned goals is essential for ensuring that all departments are working toward the same objectives. These goals should be specific, measurable, achievable, relevant, and time-bound (SMART). Moreover, they should cascade from the organization's overall strategy to departmental and individual goals. This alignment ensures that every team member understands how their contributions impact the company's success. For instance, an e-commerce company might set a company-wide goal to increase online sales by 20% in the next year. This goal would then be broken down into specific targets for the marketing, sales, and customer service departments, ensuring that all efforts are aligned.

Regular performance reviews and feedback sessions are important for maintaining alignment. These reviews should assess not only individual and departmental performance but also how well teams are working together toward common goals. Constructive feedback helps identify areas for improvement and reinforces the importance of alignment. For example, a financial services firm might conduct quarterly reviews where managers evaluate team performance and provide feedback on collaboration and goal alignment. This process helps keep everyone focused and on track.

Training and development programs can also support alignment by equipping employees with the skills and knowledge they need to work effectively across departments. These programs should include training on communication, teamwork, and project management. For example, a manufacturing company might offer workshops on effective communication and collaboration techniques for its employees. By investing in these skills, the company can enhance its overall alignment and productivity.

Creating a culture of accountability is crucial for sustaining alignment. This means holding individuals and teams responsible for their contributions and ensuring that everyone is committed to the organization's goals. Accountability can be reinforced through performance metrics, regular check-ins, and recognition programs. For instance, a hospitality company might implement a system where team members are regularly evaluated on their contributions to departmental and company-wide objectives. Recognizing and rewarding those who consistently demonstrate alignment and collaboration can further reinforce this culture.

Moreover, flexibility and adaptability are important for maintaining alignment in a dynamic business environment. Organizations must be able to adjust their strategies and goals in response to market changes, customer feedback, and other external factors. This requires a flexible approach to planning and a willingness to pivot when necessary. For example, a software company that quickly adapts its development priorities based on user feedback can ensure that its products remain relevant and aligned with customer needs.

Monitoring and measuring alignment is essential for continuous improvement. This involves regularly assessing how well departments and teams are working together and making adjustments as needed. Key performance indicators (KPIs) related to collaboration, communication, and goal achievement can provide valuable insights. For example, a logistics company might track metrics such as on-time delivery rates, customer satisfaction scores, and team collaboration ratings. By analyzing these metrics, the company can identify areas for improvement and take corrective actions.

In conclusion, aligning departments and teams is a multifaceted process that requires clear communication, strategic planning, strong leadership, and a culture of collaboration. By establishing a shared vision, promoting open communication, leveraging collaboration tools, developing cross-functional teams, setting aligned goals, conducting regular performance reviews, investing in training, fostering accountability, and maintaining flexibility, organizations can achieve a high level of alignment. This alignment not only enhances efficiency and productivity but also drives innovation, improves customer satisfaction, and contributes to long-term success. Through sustained effort and commitment, companies can create a unified and cohesive organization where all departments work together seamlessly toward common goals. Effective alignment within an organization also extends to embracing diversity and inclusion. Diverse teams bring a wealth of perspectives, ideas, and problem-solving approaches, which can significantly enhance creativity and innovation. By fostering an inclusive culture where every team member feels valued and heard, companies can ensure that all voices contribute to the collective goals. For example, a global consulting firm might implement diversity initiatives and inclusive leadership training to ensure that its teams are leveraging the full spectrum of their employees' talents and experiences.

Measuring Cultural Impact

Understanding the impact of organizational culture is essential for ensuring long-term success and employee satisfaction. Measuring cultural impact involves assessing how the shared values, beliefs, and behaviors within a company influence its operations, employee engagement, and overall performance. This process requires a combination of qualitative and quantitative methods to capture a comprehensive picture of the organizational culture.

One effective way to begin measuring cultural impact is through employee surveys. These surveys can provide valuable insights into how employees perceive the company culture and its effects on their work. Questions might address areas such as job satisfaction, alignment with company values, communication effectiveness, and perceptions of leadership. For instance, a survey could ask employees to rate their agreement with statements like, "I feel valued and respected at work," or "Leadership communicates the company's vision effectively." Analyzing the responses helps identify strengths and areas needing improvement within the culture.

Focus groups and interviews offer deeper insights into cultural impact. These methods allow for more detailed discussions and can uncover nuanced perspectives that surveys might miss. For example, a series of focus groups with employees from different departments could reveal how culture varies across the organization and highlight specific challenges or successes. Similarly, one-on-one interviews with key leaders can provide a top-down view of cultural priorities and how they are being communicated and implemented.

Observational methods are another valuable tool for measuring cultural impact. By observing interactions and behaviors within the workplace, one can gain a direct understanding of the culture in action. This might involve attending meetings, watching day-to-day operations, or shadowing employees. Observations can reveal how well the company values are embodied in everyday practices and whether there are discrepancies between stated values and actual behaviors. For instance, if a company values innovation but meetings are dominated by hierarchical decision-making, this misalignment can be identified through observation.

Analyzing organizational metrics can also provide quantitative data on cultural impact. Metrics such as employee turnover rates, absenteeism, productivity levels, and customer satisfaction scores can reflect aspects of the company culture. High turnover rates, for example, might indicate a problematic culture, while high productivity and customer satisfaction could suggest a positive, supportive environment. By correlating these metrics with cultural initiatives or changes, organizations can assess the effectiveness of their cultural strategies.

Another approach to measuring cultural impact is through cultural audits. A cultural audit is a comprehensive evaluation of the organization's culture, often conducted by an external consultant. This process typically involves a combination of surveys, interviews, focus groups, and document analysis. The goal is to provide an objective assessment of the culture and identify areas for improvement. For instance, a cultural audit might reveal that while the company promotes teamwork, its reward systems are primarily individual-based, creating a misalignment that needs addressing.

Employee engagement surveys are particularly useful for understanding the impact of culture on employee morale and productivity. These surveys measure how emotionally and mentally committed employees are to their work and the organization. Engagement surveys can include questions about job satisfaction, emotional commitment, and the likelihood of recommending the company as a great place to work. For example, an engaged workforce typically shows higher levels of productivity and lower turnover rates, indicating a positive cultural impact.

Leadership assessments are crucial for understanding how leaders influence and embody the company culture. Effective leaders should model the desired cultural attributes and inspire their teams to do the same. Leadership assessments can include 360-degree feedback, where leaders receive input from their peers, subordinates, and superiors. This feedback can highlight strengths and areas for development in how leaders are perceived to uphold and promote the company culture. For example, if leaders are rated highly in transparency and communication, it suggests a positive cultural influence.

Benchmarking against industry standards or best practices can also provide insights into cultural impact. By comparing the organization's cultural metrics with those of similar companies, one can identify areas where the company stands out or lags behind. For instance, if an organization's employee engagement scores are consistently higher than industry averages, it indicates a strong, positive culture. Conversely, lower scores suggest areas needing attention.

Case studies and storytelling can illustrate cultural impact in a more narrative format. Sharing stories of how the culture has influenced specific projects, decisions, or individual success can provide tangible examples of cultural impact. For example, a case study might describe how a collaborative culture led to a successful cross-departmental project, highlighting the benefits of the cultural approach. These stories can be powerful tools for reinforcing the desired culture and demonstrating its value to employees.

One practical example of measuring cultural impact comes from a large multinational corporation that implemented a comprehensive cultural assessment program. The company conducted annual employee surveys, focus groups, and leadership assessments to gauge cultural alignment. They also tracked key performance indicators such as employee retention, innovation rates, and customer satisfaction. Over time, they noticed a strong correlation between high engagement scores and increased innovation, leading to a strategic focus on enhancing engagement through cultural initiatives.

The organization also used storytelling to reinforce cultural values. They regularly shared success stories in company newsletters and at town hall meetings, highlighting how the culture contributed to notable achievements. This approach not only measured cultural impact but also actively shaped and strengthened the culture.

Organizations should also consider the role of external perception in measuring cultural impact. The company's reputation in the market and among potential employees can reflect its internal culture. Employer branding surveys and reviews on platforms like Glassdoor can provide insights into how the outside world perceives the company's culture. For instance, positive reviews about the work environment and leadership can attract top talent, while negative reviews might signal cultural issues needing attention.

Ultimately, the goal of measuring cultural impact is to create a feedback loop that informs continuous improvement. By regularly assessing cultural impact and making data-driven adjustments, organizations can cultivate a supportive, high-performing culture. This involves not just measuring but also acting on the findings to address gaps, celebrate successes, and align cultural initiatives with overall business strategy.

In conclusion, measuring cultural impact is a complex but essential task that requires a multifaceted approach. Through employee surveys, focus groups, observational methods, organizational metrics, cultural audits, engagement surveys, leadership assessments, benchmarking, storytelling, and external perception analysis, organizations can gain a comprehensive understanding of their culture's influence. By using these insights to drive continuous improvement, companies can ensure that their culture supports their strategic goals and fosters a positive, productive work environment. Over time, maintaining an adaptive approach to measuring cultural impact is crucial. As the organization evolves, so too will its cultural dynamics. Regularly revisiting and refining measurement tools ensures they remain relevant and effective. For example, as new technologies and work practices emerge, survey questions and observational methods might need updating to reflect these changes. Continuous learning and adaptation will help organizations stay in tune with their cultural landscape and respond proactively to shifts.

Chapter 4

Designing Customer-Centric Products and Services

Identifying Customer Needs

Understanding and identifying customer needs is crucial for any business aiming to succeed in a competitive market. This process involves recognizing both the explicit and implicit desires of customers and using that knowledge to inform product development, marketing strategies, and customer service practices. A comprehensive approach to identifying customer needs combines direct feedback, market research, and data analysis to create a well-rounded understanding of what customers truly want.

One of the most direct methods to identify customer needs is through customer surveys. Surveys can be designed to gather specific feedback on products, services, and overall customer experience. Open-ended questions in surveys allow customers to express their needs and preferences in their own words, providing valuable qualitative data. For example, asking customers, "What features would you like to see in our next product release?" can yield insights into desired improvements and innovations. To increase response rates and the quality of feedback, companies should ensure that surveys are concise, user-friendly, and incentivized when possible.

Customer interviews offer deeper insights through one-on-one conversations. These interviews can

87

uncover nuanced details about customer preferences and pain points that surveys might miss. Conducting interviews with a diverse group of customers—ranging from loyal users to those who have switched to competitors—can provide a broad perspective on customer needs. For instance, an interview might reveal that a product feature highly valued by loyal customers is not well-communicated in marketing materials, suggesting a need for better messaging.

Focus groups are another effective tool for identifying customer needs. These moderated discussions with a small group of customers can generate rich qualitative data and foster dynamic conversations that reveal collective preferences and attitudes. In focus groups, customers can discuss their experiences with a product or service, compare it with competitors, and suggest improvements. For example, a focus group discussing a new software product might highlight a common desire for a more intuitive user interface, leading to design changes that enhance user satisfaction.

Analyzing customer feedback from various channels—such as social media, online reviews, and customer service interactions—provides a wealth of information on customer needs. Social media platforms, in particular, offer real-time insights into customer opinions and trends. Monitoring mentions of the brand, products, and industry hashtags can help identify emerging trends and common pain points. For instance, if multiple customers on Twitter mention difficulties with a product feature, it signals a need for improvement or additional user support.

Sales and customer service teams are on the front lines of customer interaction and can provide valuable insights into customer needs. Regularly consulting with these teams and gathering their observations can reveal patterns and recurring issues faced by customers. For example, if the sales team frequently encounters questions about a specific product feature, this might indicate a need for better product education or adjustments to the feature itself.

Market research, including competitor analysis, helps identify customer needs by examining industry trends and the offerings of other companies. Understanding what competitors are doing well—and where they fall short—can highlight opportunities for differentiation and improvement. For instance, if a competitor's product is praised for its user-friendly design, but customers complain about its limited functionality, there might be an opportunity to develop a product that combines ease of use with robust features.

Customer journey mapping is a strategic tool that visualizes the steps customers take when interacting with a company, from initial awareness to post-purchase support. Mapping the customer journey helps identify key touchpoints where customer needs and expectations are highest. By analyzing these touchpoints, businesses can pinpoint areas for improvement and innovation. For example, if the journey map reveals that customers often abandon their shopping carts at the payment stage, it may indicate a need for a more streamlined checkout process.

Behavioral data analysis provides objective insights into customer needs based on actual usage patterns and interactions. By analyzing data from websites, mobile apps, and other digital platforms, businesses can identify trends and preferences that might not be explicitly stated by customers. For example, if data shows that users frequently access a particular feature of an app, it suggests that this feature is highly valued and should be prioritized in future updates.

Customer personas are fictional representations of ideal customers based on demographic data, behavior patterns, and psychographic insights. Creating detailed personas helps businesses understand the needs, goals, and challenges of different customer segments. For instance, a persona for a tech-savvy young professional might highlight a need for advanced features and seamless integration with other devices, guiding product development and marketing strategies to cater to this segment.

Empathy mapping is a technique used to gain a deeper understanding of customer experiences by exploring what customers think, feel, say, and do. This method helps identify emotional drivers and barriers that influence customer behavior. For example, an empathy map might reveal that customers feel frustrated by lengthy support wait times, suggesting a need for improved customer service processes.

Prototyping and testing are iterative processes that involve creating early versions of a product and gathering feedback from customers. This hands-on approach helps identify customer needs by observing how users interact with a prototype and where they encounter difficulties. For instance, testing a new app feature with a small group of users can reveal usability issues and areas for enhancement before a full-scale launch.

Listening to customer stories and testimonials provides authentic insights into how customers use and perceive products. These stories often highlight needs and challenges that may not be captured through formal research methods. For example, a customer testimonial might describe a creative way they use a product, revealing a new use case that can be explored and marketed.

Co-creation involves collaborating with customers in the development process, inviting them to contribute ideas and feedback. This participatory approach ensures that products and services are closely aligned with customer needs. For instance, hosting a design workshop where customers can brainstorm and prototype new product features can lead to innovative solutions that directly address customer desires.

Finally, staying attuned to broader societal and technological trends can help anticipate future customer needs. By monitoring shifts in consumer behavior, emerging technologies, and cultural trends, businesses can proactively adapt to changing customer expectations. For example, the growing emphasis on sustainability might prompt a company to develop eco-friendly products in response to increasing environmental consciousness among customers.

In conclusion, identifying customer needs requires a multifaceted approach that combines direct feedback, data analysis, and proactive engagement. By leveraging surveys, interviews, focus groups, social media monitoring, and other methods, businesses can gain a comprehensive understanding of what their customers truly want. This understanding not only informs product development and marketing strategies but also enhances customer satisfaction and loyalty. Through continuous learning and adaptation, businesses can stay ahead of evolving customer needs and maintain a competitive edge in the market. Understanding customer needs is not a one-time effort but a continuous process that requires consistent attention and adaptation. Businesses must remain agile and responsive to changing customer expectations, market dynamics, and technological advancements. This ongoing commitment to understanding and meeting customer needs can drive innovation, improve customer satisfaction, and ultimately lead to long-term success.

Co-Creation with Customers

Co-creation with customers represents a transformative approach to business that actively involves customers in the development of products and services. This collaborative process not only enhances the relevance and appeal of offerings but also fosters a deeper connection between businesses and their customers. By inviting customers to participate in ideation, design, and testing, companies can tap into the collective creativity and insights of their user base, leading to innovative solutions that resonate more closely with market needs.

One of the foundational steps in co-creation is to identify and engage a diverse group of customers who represent various segments of the target market. This diversity ensures that the feedback and ideas gathered are comprehensive and inclusive, addressing the needs and preferences of a broad audience. For example, a company developing a new smartphone might include tech enthusiasts, casual users, and older adults in its co-creation process to ensure the final product appeals to a wide range of users.

To facilitate effective co-creation, businesses must create an environment that encourages open communication and collaboration. This can be achieved through workshops, focus groups, online forums, and collaborative platforms where customers can freely share their ideas and feedback. For instance, a fashion brand might host a series of design workshops where customers can brainstorm and sketch new clothing concepts alongside professional designers. These sessions not only generate fresh ideas but also allow customers to feel a sense of ownership and involvement in the brand.

Leveraging technology can significantly enhance the co-creation experience. Online platforms and tools enable real-time collaboration and feedback, making it easier for customers to participate regardless of their location. Companies can use social media, dedicated co-creation websites, and mobile apps to gather input and facilitate discussions. For example, a software company could use an online platform to allow users to suggest and vote on new features, creating a dynamic and interactive co-creation process.

Transparency and trust are crucial elements in successful co-creation. Customers need to feel that their contributions are valued and that the business is genuinely committed to incorporating their feedback. Regular updates on the progress of the project and how customer input is being used can help build this trust. For instance, a car manufacturer might provide regular video updates showing how customer feedback is influencing the design of a new vehicle model, thus keeping participants engaged and informed throughout the development process.

Incentives can also play a key role in encouraging customer participation in co-creation. Offering rewards such as discounts, exclusive previews, or recognition in the final product can motivate customers to contribute their time and ideas. For example, a gaming company might offer beta testers exclusive in-game items or early access to new features as a thank-you for their feedback and participation.

Co-creation can extend beyond product development to include marketing and branding efforts. By involving customers in the creation of marketing campaigns, companies can ensure that their messaging resonates more deeply with the target audience. For instance, a beverage company might run a campaign inviting customers to submit their own commercials or social media posts featuring the product, with the best entries being used in official marketing efforts. This approach not only generates authentic content but also builds a community of brand advocates.

One of the significant benefits of co-creation is the ability to rapidly prototype and iterate on ideas. By involving customers early in the development process, companies can quickly identify what works and what doesn't, making adjustments before significant resources are invested. For example, a tech startup might release a series of prototypes to a group of beta users, gathering feedback and making improvements at each stage. This iterative process ensures that the final product is well-aligned with customer expectations and needs.

The insights gained from co-creation can also lead to unexpected innovations. Customers often use products in ways that designers might not anticipate, and their creative solutions can inspire new features or entirely new products. For instance, a kitchen appliance manufacturer might discover through co-creation workshops that customers are using a blender for a variety of unconventional purposes, leading to the development of new accessories or multifunctional features.

To maximize the impact of co-creation, businesses should integrate the process into their overall innovation strategy. This means not only using customer input for individual projects but also creating a culture that values and seeks out customer collaboration at every level. For example, a company might establish a dedicated co-creation team responsible for facilitating customer involvement across different departments, ensuring that the insights and ideas generated are effectively used to drive innovation and growth.

Measuring the success of co-creation efforts is essential to understand their impact and improve future initiatives. Metrics such as customer satisfaction, engagement levels, and the success of co-created products in the market can provide valuable feedback. For example, a company might track the performance of a co-created product compared to traditionally developed ones, analyzing factors such as sales, customer reviews, and retention rates to assess the effectiveness of the co-creation process.

The story of LEGO provides a powerful example of successful co-creation. Facing declining sales in the early 2000s, the company turned to its passionate user base for ideas. Through initiatives like the LEGO Ideas platform, where fans can submit and vote on new set designs, LEGO tapped into the creativity of its community. This not only led to popular new products but also strengthened the bond between the brand and its customers. The success of co-created sets like the LEGO NASA Apollo Saturn V and the LEGO Ghostbusters Ecto-1 demonstrates the potential of customer collaboration.

While co-creation offers numerous benefits, it also presents challenges. Managing diverse opinions and balancing customer desires with practical constraints requires careful planning and communication. Businesses must be prepared to navigate conflicts and ensure that the co-creation process remains productive and focused. For example, a company might employ skilled moderators in online forums or workshops to facilitate discussions and keep the group aligned on common goals.

In conclusion, co-creation with customers is a powerful strategy for driving innovation, enhancing product relevance, and building stronger customer relationships. By actively involving customers in the development process, businesses can tap into a wealth of creativity and insights that might otherwise go untapped. This collaborative approach not only leads to more successful products but also fosters a sense of community and loyalty among customers. To achieve these benefits, businesses must create an environment that encourages open communication, leverage technology to facilitate collaboration, and integrate co-creation into their overall innovation strategy. Through careful planning and execution, co-creation can become a cornerstone of a company's success, ensuring that its offerings continually evolve to meet the changing needs and desires of its customers. Incorporating co-creation into a business's core operations also requires a shift in mindset. Traditionally, companies have viewed themselves as the primary creators and customers as passive consumers. Co-creation flips this dynamic, positioning customers as active partners in the creation process. This shift demands a more open and flexible organizational culture where customer input is not just welcomed but actively sought and integrated.

Prototyping and Testing

Prototyping and testing are critical stages in the product development process, offering a structured approach to transforming ideas into tangible solutions. By iterating through these phases, businesses can identify and rectify potential issues, ensuring that the final product meets both user needs and quality standards. The journey from concept to market-ready product is fraught with challenges, but effective prototyping and testing can significantly mitigate risks and enhance the overall success of the product.

The first step in prototyping is to create a preliminary version of the product, often referred to as a low-fidelity prototype. This initial model is typically simple and inexpensive, focusing on the core functionality rather than aesthetics. For instance, a low-fidelity prototype of a new mobile app might be a series of hand-drawn sketches or a basic wireframe that outlines the main user interface elements and navigation flow. The goal at this stage is to quickly bring ideas to life and facilitate early feedback.

Gathering feedback from potential users and stakeholders is crucial once the low-fidelity prototype is ready. This feedback helps to validate assumptions, uncover unforeseen issues, and gauge initial reactions. Techniques such as user interviews, surveys, and observation can provide valuable insights. For example, a startup developing a wearable fitness tracker might invite a group of fitness enthusiasts to test the prototype and share their thoughts on its usability and functionality. This feedback can highlight areas for improvement and guide subsequent iterations.

As the design evolves, the next step is to create a high-fidelity prototype. This version is more polished and closer to the final product in terms of appearance and functionality. It might include detailed graphics, interactive elements, and more refined features. For a physical product, a high-fidelity prototype could be a 3D-printed model that closely resembles the intended final version. High-fidelity prototypes are essential for conducting more rigorous testing and obtaining more accurate feedback.

Testing is an integral part of the prototyping process, ensuring that the product performs as expected and meets user needs. There are several types of testing, each serving a different purpose. Usability testing focuses on how easily users can interact with the product. During usability testing, participants are asked to complete specific tasks while observers note any difficulties or confusion. For example, a software company might conduct usability testing for a new app by asking users to navigate through various features and provide feedback on their experience.

Functional testing, on the other hand, assesses whether the product functions correctly and meets the specified requirements. This type of testing is particularly important for identifying bugs or technical issues that could affect performance. For instance, a tech company developing a new smart home device might run a series of functional tests to ensure that it connects properly to Wi-Fi, responds accurately to commands, and integrates seamlessly with other smart devices.

Performance testing evaluates how well the product performs under different conditions, such as varying loads or stress levels. This is especially important for products expected to handle high volumes of users or data. For example, an e-commerce platform might conduct performance testing to ensure that its website remains fast and responsive during peak shopping periods. This testing helps identify potential bottlenecks and areas for optimization.

Another crucial aspect of testing is user acceptance testing (UAT), where the final product is tested by the end-users in a real-world environment. UAT helps ensure that the product meets the users' needs and expectations before it is launched to the broader market. For instance, a financial software company might deploy its new accounting tool to a select group of accountants to use in their daily work, gathering feedback and making final adjustments based on their experiences.

Iterative testing and prototyping are essential to the development process, allowing for continuous refinement and improvement. Each round of testing provides new insights, leading to further iterations of the prototype. This cycle of feedback and improvement helps ensure that the final product is both high-quality and user-centric. For example, a medical device company might go through multiple rounds of prototyping and testing to ensure that its new device is safe, effective, and easy to use for healthcare professionals.

Collaboration is key during the prototyping and testing phases. Involving cross-functional teams, including designers, engineers, marketers, and potential users, ensures that diverse perspectives are considered. This collaborative approach can lead to more innovative solutions and a more comprehensive understanding of potential issues. For example, a consumer electronics company might bring together its design, engineering, and customer support teams to work on a new product, ensuring that all aspects of the user experience are considered and optimized.

Prototyping and testing also play a vital role in risk management. By identifying and addressing potential issues early in the development process, businesses can avoid costly mistakes and delays later on. For instance, a car manufacturer might use crash testing to identify and rectify safety issues before the vehicle goes into mass production. This proactive approach helps ensure that the final product meets safety standards and regulatory requirements.

To effectively manage the prototyping and testing process, businesses can adopt various tools and methodologies. Agile development, for example, emphasizes iterative progress and continuous feedback, making it well-suited for prototyping and testing. In an Agile framework, development is broken down into small, manageable increments, with each iteration building on the previous one. This approach allows for ongoing testing and refinement, ensuring that the final product is well-aligned with user needs.

Design thinking is another valuable methodology that emphasizes empathy, experimentation, and iteration. By focusing on understanding the user's perspective and experimenting with different solutions, design thinking encourages a user-centric approach to prototyping and testing. For example, a healthcare company might use design thinking to develop a new patient monitoring system, involving patients and healthcare providers in the design process to ensure that the system is intuitive and effective.

Digital tools such as computer-aided design (CAD) software, 3D printing, and simulation software can also enhance the prototyping and testing process. These tools allow for rapid prototyping, detailed visualization, and accurate testing of different scenarios. For example, an aerospace company might use CAD software to create detailed models of a new aircraft component, then use simulation software to test its performance under various conditions before producing a physical prototype.

Documenting the prototyping and testing process is essential for maintaining a clear record of decisions, changes, and feedback. Detailed documentation helps ensure that all team members are aligned and that valuable insights are captured for future reference. For instance, a pharmaceutical company might maintain detailed records of its drug development process, including test results, feedback from clinical trials, and regulatory compliance documentation. This documentation not only supports the current project but also provides a valuable knowledge base for future developments.

Prototyping and testing are dynamic and iterative processes that are central to successful product development. By creating early prototypes, gathering user feedback, and conducting thorough testing, businesses can refine their ideas and ensure that the final product meets user needs and quality standards. The collaborative nature of prototyping and testing fosters innovation and helps mitigate risks, leading to more successful and user-centric products. Through careful planning, execution, and a commitment to continuous improvement, businesses can harness the power of prototyping and testing to drive innovation and achieve their development goals. In addition to the methods and tools previously mentioned, embracing a culture of experimentation within the organization can significantly enhance the prototyping and testing phases. Encouraging team members to test out new ideas, even if they seem unconventional, can lead to groundbreaking innovations. This culture of experimentation promotes a mindset where failure is seen as a learning opportunity rather than a setback.

Iterative Design Processes

Iterative design processes form the backbone of successful product development, allowing teams to refine their ideas through repeated cycles of prototyping, testing, and evaluation. This approach contrasts sharply with linear methods, which often lead to rigid and less user-centric outcomes. By embracing iteration, designers and developers can adapt to feedback, uncover hidden issues, and ultimately create more effective and user-friendly products.

The iterative design process begins with understanding the problem or opportunity at hand. This involves thorough research to gather insights into user needs, market conditions, and technological possibilities. For example, a company developing a new kitchen appliance might start by conducting surveys and interviews with potential users to understand their cooking habits, pain points, and desired features. This user research forms the foundation for the initial design concept.

Once the problem is well-defined, the team moves on to brainstorming and ideation. This phase is characterized by creative thinking and the generation of multiple concepts. It's important to encourage diverse perspectives and ideas during this stage, as they can lead to innovative solutions. Techniques such as sketching, mind mapping, and collaborative workshops can help generate a wide range of concepts. For instance, an automotive company designing a new electric vehicle might hold brainstorming sessions with engineers, designers, and market analysts to explore various design directions and features.

After generating a pool of ideas, the next step is to create low-fidelity prototypes of the most promising concepts. These early prototypes are usually simple and inexpensive, focusing on key functionalities rather than detailed aesthetics. They serve as tangible representations of the ideas, making it easier to communicate and test them. For example, a tech startup developing a new mobile app might create wireframes or mockups to visualize the app's layout and navigation. These low-fidelity prototypes are then tested with potential users to gather initial feedback.

User feedback is a crucial component of the iterative design process. By observing how users interact with the prototype and listening to their feedback, designers can identify strengths and weaknesses. This feedback loop is essential for making informed decisions about which aspects of the design to keep, modify, or discard. For instance, a team working on a wearable fitness tracker might discover through user testing that the interface is confusing, prompting them to simplify the design.

Based on the feedback received, the team refines the prototype, adding more details and improving functionality. This results in a higher-fidelity prototype, which is again tested with users. This cycle of prototyping, testing, and refinement continues until the product meets the desired quality and usability standards. Each iteration brings the product closer to its final form, incorporating user insights and addressing issues that arise during testing. For example, an educational software company might go through several iterations of its learning platform, gradually enhancing the user experience and adding new features based on student and teacher feedback.

Iterative design processes also benefit from cross-functional collaboration. Involving team members from different disciplines—such as design, engineering, marketing, and customer support—ensures that various perspectives are considered throughout development. This multidisciplinary approach helps identify potential challenges early on and fosters innovative solutions. For instance, a healthcare company developing a new medical device might include input from doctors, nurses, engineers, and regulatory experts to ensure the device is effective, safe, and compliant with regulations.

While the iterative design process is inherently flexible, it requires careful planning and management to be effective. Setting clear goals and timelines for each iteration helps keep the project on track and ensures steady progress. Regular check-ins and reviews with the team can help identify any roadblocks and keep everyone aligned. For example, a project manager overseeing the development of a new consumer electronics product might hold weekly meetings to review the latest prototype, discuss feedback, and plan the next steps.

Documentation is another important aspect of the iterative design process. Keeping detailed records of each iteration, including design changes, user feedback, and testing results, provides a valuable reference for future development. This documentation helps the team track progress, understand the rationale behind design decisions, and avoid repeating past mistakes. For instance, a software development team might use a project management tool to document each iteration of their application, including user stories, bug reports, and feature updates.

Iterative design processes also encourage a culture of continuous improvement. By regularly revisiting and refining the product, teams can adapt to changing user needs and market conditions. This mindset of constant iteration and enhancement is crucial for maintaining a competitive edge. For example, a social media platform might continuously update its features and interface based on user feedback and emerging trends, ensuring it remains relevant and engaging.

However, iterative design is not without its challenges. One common pitfall is the risk of scope creep, where the project expands beyond its original goals due to ongoing changes and additions. To mitigate this risk, it's important to maintain a clear focus on the core objectives and prioritize features accordingly. Establishing a well-defined scope and sticking to it can help prevent the project from becoming unmanageable. For example, a game development team might set strict milestones for each iteration, ensuring they stay on track while still incorporating user feedback.

Another challenge is balancing speed and quality. While quick iterations are important for maintaining momentum, it's equally crucial to ensure that each iteration is thoroughly tested and refined. Rushing through iterations without proper testing can lead to subpar results and missed opportunities for improvement. For instance, a startup developing a new software tool might allocate sufficient time for each testing phase, ensuring that user feedback is accurately captured and addressed.

The iterative design process can also benefit from leveraging digital tools and technologies. Software such as computer-aided design (CAD), 3D printing, and prototyping platforms can streamline the creation and testing of prototypes. These tools enable rapid iteration and provide precise control over design changes. For example, an industrial design team might use CAD software to quickly iterate on the design of a new consumer product, creating detailed models that can be easily modified and tested.

In conclusion, iterative design processes are essential for developing successful products. By embracing iteration, teams can continuously refine their ideas, incorporate user feedback, and adapt to changing conditions. This approach fosters innovation, improves usability, and reduces the risk of costly mistakes. Through careful planning, cross-functional collaboration, and a commitment to continuous improvement, businesses can harness the power of iterative design to create products that truly resonate with users. Iteration also helps in uncovering unforeseen issues that might not be evident in the initial stages of design. These issues can range from technical challenges to user experience problems that only become apparent when the product is in use. For example, a company developing a new type of ergonomic office chair might discover through iterative testing that certain materials wear out faster than expected, prompting a switch to more durable alternatives.

Launching and Monitoring Products

Bringing a product to market and monitoring its performance is a dynamic and multifaceted process that requires strategic planning, execution, and ongoing vigilance. Launching a product successfully involves understanding your market, preparing a comprehensive go-to-market strategy, and ensuring that all aspects of the launch are seamlessly coordinated. Once the product is launched, continuous monitoring is essential to gauge its performance, understand user feedback, and make necessary adjustments. This chapter delves into the practical steps and considerations to ensure a successful product launch and effective post-launch monitoring.

Before launching a product, it's crucial to conduct thorough market research. This involves identifying your target audience, understanding their needs, and analyzing the competitive landscape. Market research provides insights into potential market size, customer preferences, and the strengths and weaknesses of competitors. For instance, if you're launching a new fitness app, you might survey potential users to understand their fitness goals, preferred features, and the types of workouts they enjoy. This information helps in tailoring the product to meet user needs and differentiating it from existing solutions.

With a clear understanding of the market, the next step is to develop a comprehensive go-to-market strategy. This strategy outlines how the product will be positioned, marketed, and sold. It includes defining the unique selling proposition (USP), setting pricing strategies, and planning promotional activities. The USP highlights what makes the product unique and why customers should choose it over competitors. For example, a new organic skincare line might emphasize its use of natural ingredients and eco-friendly packaging as its USP. Pricing strategy is also critical; it involves setting a price that reflects the product's value while remaining competitive. Promotional activities could include digital marketing campaigns, influencer partnerships, and public relations efforts to generate buzz and awareness.

Effective product positioning is key to a successful launch. This involves crafting a compelling brand story and message that resonates with your target audience. The brand story should communicate the product's value, benefits, and the problem it solves. For instance, a tech startup launching a smart home device might position it as a way to simplify daily tasks and enhance home security. The messaging should be consistent across all marketing channels, including the website, social media, and advertising campaigns.

A successful product launch requires meticulous planning and coordination. This includes setting a launch date, preparing marketing materials, and ensuring that all logistical aspects are in place. It's important to create a detailed launch plan that outlines key milestones, responsibilities, and timelines. For example, a fashion brand launching a new clothing line might plan a series of events leading up to the launch, such as teaser campaigns, influencer previews, and a grand launch event. Coordination with retailers, suppliers, and other partners is also crucial to ensure that the product is available and accessible to customers at launch.

As the launch date approaches, it's essential to build anticipation and excitement. Pre-launch activities can include teaser campaigns, early access offers, and engaging content that piques interest. Social media is a powerful tool for generating buzz and engaging with potential customers. For example, a gaming company launching a new video game might release trailers, behind-the-scenes content, and exclusive previews to build excitement among fans. Offering early access or limited-time discounts can also incentivize early adopters and create a sense of urgency.

On the day of the launch, all efforts should come together seamlessly. This includes ensuring that the product is available for purchase, marketing campaigns are live, and customer support is ready to handle inquiries. It's important to monitor the launch closely and be prepared to address any issues that arise. For instance, an e-commerce platform launching a new product line should have systems in place to handle increased traffic and ensure a smooth purchasing experience. Real-time monitoring can help identify and resolve any technical glitches or customer service issues quickly.

Post-launch monitoring is critical to understanding how the product is performing and identifying areas for improvement. This involves tracking key performance indicators (KPIs) such as sales, customer feedback, and market penetration. Sales data provides insights into how well the product is being received and whether it's meeting revenue targets. Customer feedback, gathered through reviews, surveys, and direct interactions, offers valuable insights into user satisfaction and areas for enhancement. For example, a software company might use customer feedback to identify bugs, usability issues, and feature requests.

Analyzing market penetration helps assess the product's reach and market share. This involves comparing the product's performance against competitors and understanding its position in the market. For instance, a new beverage brand might track its distribution and sales in various regions to understand where it's gaining traction and where additional marketing efforts are needed. This analysis can inform future marketing strategies and help in making data-driven decisions.

Continuous improvement is a key aspect of post-launch monitoring. By regularly reviewing performance data and customer feedback, companies can identify opportunities for product enhancements and updates. This iterative approach ensures that the product remains relevant and competitive in the market. For example, a mobile app might release regular updates based on user feedback to improve functionality, add new features, and fix bugs. Engaging with customers and showing that their feedback is valued can also enhance brand loyalty and user satisfaction.

Effective communication and engagement with customers are essential throughout the launch and post-launch phases. This involves maintaining an active presence on social media, responding to customer inquiries, and providing timely updates. Transparency and responsiveness build trust and can help address any concerns or issues promptly. For instance, a consumer electronics company launching a new gadget might use social media to address common questions, share tips and tutorials, and highlight positive customer experiences. Creating a community around the product can also foster loyalty and advocacy.

Monitoring competitors is another important aspect of post-launch activities. Understanding how competitors are responding to your product and what strategies they are employing can provide valuable insights. This competitive analysis helps in identifying potential threats and opportunities in the market. For example, a new entrant in the streaming service industry might monitor competitors' pricing changes, content offerings, and marketing campaigns to stay ahead and refine their own strategies.

In summary, launching a product successfully and monitoring its performance requires a strategic and well-coordinated approach. Comprehensive market research, a clear go-to-market strategy, and effective positioning are crucial for a successful launch. Building anticipation and excitement through pre-launch activities and ensuring a seamless launch day are essential for capturing customer interest. Post-launch monitoring, including tracking KPIs, analyzing customer feedback, and staying informed about competitors, is vital for continuous improvement and maintaining a competitive edge. By following these steps and remaining adaptable, companies can navigate the complexities of product launches and achieve long-term success in the market. Additionally, leveraging data analytics is a powerful way to refine product strategies post-launch. In the digital age, the abundance of data from various channels—such as social media, website analytics, and customer interactions—can provide deep insights into user behavior and preferences. By using advanced analytics tools, companies can track how customers are interacting with the product, identify patterns, and predict future trends. For instance, an e-commerce business can analyze user behavior on its website to understand which products are most popular, what navigation paths lead to successful purchases, and where users drop off in the purchasing process. This data-driven approach enables businesses to make informed decisions and optimize their product offerings and marketing strategies.